RECOGNIZING THE REAL ENEMY

ACCURATELY DISCERNING THE ARMY OF DARKNESS

By

Miguel A. Demelli

Additional copies of this book may be obtained at:
www.recognizingtheenemy.com.

This book is **also available in Spanish** under the title
"Reconociendo Al Verdadero Enemigo" and may also be
obtained at: www.recognizingtheenemy.com.

All Scripture quotations are from the King James Version of
the Bible.

Some Scripture passages are underlined by the author for
emphasis.

Rev. 2A-20120119

ISBN: 978-160844-157-0

Printed in the USA by 48HrBooks (www.48HrBooks.com)

ABOUT THE COVER

"Under His Wings"

Shortly before departing for a conference in St. Louis, MO. in August 2008, I suddenly realized that this book was almost ready for a cover but I had none. I briefly wondered how this would be resolved. I thought about it for a moment and remembered that, just as God had foreknown everything, He had already planned and provided the cover that this book was supposed to have. So, I prayed briefly and rested in knowing that He would simply "show me" and let me know, whenever He would bring me across it. I had also asked Him to show me an image of what the cover should be like.

Only days later, on the last morning of the conference, I came across **Rosemary Burke**'s tables at the marketplace. She had a wide array of prints, artwork and other items. For some reason, I felt led to stop and browse...and immediately my eyes stopped upon the print you see on this book's cover (except for small changes). I "was detained" by it.

As I looked, I was realizing several things, all at once, almost as if in slow motion. I looked up at the artist, Rosemary, and said to her: *"you have no idea what this picture is doing to me"*. I slowly understood that *"this is it, this is the cover"*. It had the right colors and hues I had seen and imagined. It had the theme of battle and warfare. It had the "right look" and even the right shapes! I even have a statue that depicts an Israeli soldier, bowing and bearing the Israeli flag, which has the same colors, hues, shape of the helmet and is facing in the same direction as the print I was staring at. **And, most of all, it epitomizes what this book is about: that a war has been declared against us, and only *"under His wings"* can we hope to achieve victory and survival**.

Through the next few months, she patiently worked with me on how to adapt her artwork for this cover. We became good friends and also discussed this book at great length.

I am honored to benefit from the work of such a fine and accomplished artist for this cover. The least I can do is honor her and recommend her.

Thanks again, Rosemary. May Yahweh richly bless you and keep you.

DEDICATION

To my Father in Heaven, the Creator of the Universe, the One before Whom I walk, Who somehow saw fit to bestow upon me what is too wonderful for words, and which I do not deserve: a calling and a purpose, plus endless love, mercy and forgiveness. To walk and talk with me, and speak to me directly, is too marvelous to comprehend. To hear You, and to be spoken to plainly by You, is a gift beyond compare...for which I will never be able to thank You adequately. Thank You for everything. And thank You for putting it within me to bring forth this book and everything that is within me. It has all been of You! And, I offer this book as an offering to You, as my reasonable service and duty to you. May it be pleasing unto You!

To the many wonderful people that have had a hand in helping, shaping, molding and encouraging me along the way...*you know who you are...*

And, to the myriads of people that are being killed, stolen from or destroyed in some way by the armies of darkness. I pray that what has been given me to learn and to realize is **explained here, plainly and with His anointing**, so that it may proclaim liberty to the captives, set at liberty them that are bruised, bring recovery of sight to the physically **and spiritually** blind, and heal the brokenhearted...for that is the will of the Father, made possible by the unparalleled sacrifice and victory of our Messiah, through the power of the Holy Spirit...

May the King of Kings and Lord of Lords be glorified in everything we've been called to be...

ACKNOWLEDGMENTS

Special credit is given unto **Pastor Henry W. Wright**.

As specifically mentioned in Chapter 9, much of what I share in this book was first encountered and learned through the ministry of Pastor Henry, his book *"A More Excellent Way"* and the two weeks of ministry received in Thomaston, GA.

It is hereby acknowledged, with much gratitude, that Pastor Henry's ministry, ***Be In Health*™**, his books and his ministry programs have been of great blessing to me personally (as they have been for so many) and were greatly used by the Father to not only heal my soul in 2005 but also to transform and help stabilize my walk with Him ever since.

The principles taught by Pastor Henry, particularly the topics known as **"Separation"** and **"Spirit World Realities"**, have formed the foundation upon which the Holy One has continued to deepen and reveal my understanding of *what is truly afflicting us as believers and as human beings.*

Although this book is my own presentation and is filled with personal insights, understandings and revelations, it is only right to candidly admit that the fundamental principles and truths that are expanded upon in this book are based upon the wonderful things that have been learned through the ministry of Pastor Henry. Some of his principles are included here, undisguised, and clearly attributed to him.

Therefore, honor is due and rendered upon Pastor Henry for his service to the Body of Messiah; we thank the Father for his life and ministry.

Thanks are also given to **Dr. Myles Munroe** for his various books and his service to the Body of Believers. In particular, his books *"In Pursuit of Purpose"*, *"Understanding Your Potential"* and *"Releasing Your Potential"* have been of much blessing and greatly used by the Father to open my eyes and help me understand the calling and purpose that God deposited in me since the foundation of the world.

Special thanks to Illustrator **Rosemary Burke** for her gracious artistic talents and input on the cover and to **Charlotte Lewin** for her patient computer work on finalizing the cover for both the English and the Spanish versions of this book.

CONTENTS

PREFACE

A good question might be *"who are you to write such a book as this?"*

It is not an entirely unfair question. If asked in fairness, I believe the answer will satisfy. But if asked with cynicism and contempt, those very conditions in the heart of the person asking will likely not allow the answer to even seem like an answer.

The answer begins with: I am simply "a reluctant warrior"; a "reluctant soldier", **who figured out, and unto whom were revealed, a few very important things...the hard way**. I did not ask for this war. The war found me. But now that it found me, I will fight it.

Actually, I have no choice.

I am simply someone who was found by God many years ago, as I asked for Him to reveal Himself if He was real. Well, He arranged it all and He revealed Himself when He ordained that I would ask **in earnest.** Since then, I have sought to understand His ways and to find how to be victorious in and through Him. I did not realize that everything except Him in me would have to die first, or that it would not be painless.

I am simply someone who has been through many terrible failures, even those described in this book. I failed so badly, in fact, that I told God I could not go on anymore and that His plans for me simply could not possibly come to pass. I was dead and irretrievably broken and I told Him so more than once. In fact, I used the term "*squashed*".

And then, He gently but firmly replied, "*What is inside you cannot be squashed*". Ah...His voice. It was perfectly solid, without a shadow or hint of weakness or vulnerability; like a rock, and yet, gentle; loving, assuring, encouraging, inspiring...even to someone who was "*squashed*".

And yet, more failures came. I'd get up, fall down, get up, walk and even run, then fall down again. And then, I had my own "World Trade Center experience" in my life. For a while, I did not even fully know what was happening or what had just happened or who had done it. And, in the wreckage and the aftermath, I was now really sure I could not go on. All had been cancelled. All had been destroyed. All had been stolen and taken away. I had nothing left. And I was nothing. Too much had happened. It was all ruined for good. Things had gone too far.

It was then, out of the ashes, that He began to show me what had really happened, and **how** it had all happened, more precisely than ever. A strategy with several factors had been planned and then executed, piece by piece, until that strategy culminated in my "World Trade Center experience".

And, after He had revealed to me in detail how this pattern of strategy is, and has long been, at work against mankind and his relationships, He said to me that I had had a "front row seat" in this "theater" during those years and therefore, I had now learned much...by going through it with Him.

He then clearly said that it was now given unto me to write about it.

It has been given unto me to explain it, to dissect it, to uncover it and to proclaim it to all who would have the ears to hear. Often, one cannot understand an explanation unless one has had **enough** preparation for it. And I know that some have and some have not. I have realized this through several encounters.

I have already been proclaiming and explaining these truths to many for a few years now. Some have not understood them. Some have simply ignored them; others have downright mocked, resisted or even attacked them...*and me!* **But, praise God, many more have been delivered and set free from many "invisible enemies" that they never recognized before! Many were "stuck", like me, until these truths "opened our eyes" and made all the difference!**

I am humbled, and praise God, in being able to report that there are many marriages and individuals walking around today who are no longer as blind or undiscerning of many of the devices of the enemy as they once were. They are no longer as unaware of what (or whom) is hitting them or how; they now **discern** and take more effective action against **evil spiritual soldiers** (instead of people) that come to try to cause contention, strife, depression, and defeats in their lives. They are no longer "fighting with their eyes closed". They can now resist more effectively than ever. And for that, the praise is completely God's, for, as I often say: "it is He alone Who gives **revelation** about the **information** that I may share".

These explanations and illustrations have been born and refined through many "parking lot discussions" and "midnight hour talks" with many of His precious people, some blinder than others to these truths, just as I had once been "blind as a bat", despite everything that "I knew". Through these discussions and the many situations in which His insights were revealed, the Lord so graciously and definitively explained and revealed to me so much of **how these things really work**. One day I would go through something with someone...and the next morning He'd explain it completely and I'd be utterly amazed. And, He'd also "sew up my cuts from the previous night"!

One time, He actually said *"I'm glad it happened!"* I asked: *"How can you say that? It was very unpleasant!"* He simply replied, in His perfect composure: *"Now you know where they are leaking".* And so began another Shabbat morning of tremendous, detailed revelations from Him about what is at work in and between us in His Body of Believers! Most of these experiences are recorded in my prayer journals with date, time and place: several "composition notebooks" containing my "adventures with God", along with my sufferings and tears as well.

It was through a concentrated series of such events that this book was finally birthed. It was during the first hours of January 2008 that His

greatest clarifications to my understanding, received since the first days of January 2007 and throughout that year, began to flow out onto my keyboard. And now, since the first hours of 2009, the final touches are being put into this book. Most of it has been written since early 2008...but serious hindrances have continued to come against the completion of this book. I have had to fight harder than ever, using the very tools and principles from His Word that are explained here, to even make it to this point. Several times while writing in 2008, I realized just how odious this book is to the army of darkness, for they have truly fought hard to abort it and kill me. It's as if some "spiritual fatwa" had been put out on me...and that's even through the Body of Believers, as well as directly against me without any human vessels. It's as if this book was an exposé on some terrorist army in the natural!

Do I say this with any pride? Absolutely not; I say it with soberness, resignation, and even reluctance. I did not ask for this "assignment". I even wanted to quit many times. But it is true, as He said: *"what is inside you cannot be squashed"*. I finally accepted that and it is why I keep walking ahead...like a dead man...who knows I am being kept and kept alive only by the Almighty...until "my time" does finally come...regardless of who criticizes or approves, for only His opinion and approval matters.

So, I might as well "get with the program". The sooner a soldier in war comes to terms with the possibility of dying, the sooner he will be able to function like he is supposed to.

That frees him from excessive efforts at self-preservation, which only cloud and interfere with a soldier's judgment. And, whosoever seeks to save his life shall lose it...but whosoever loses his life...shall find it.

Maybe I found mine after dying enough times, only to realize that He has not let me die yet...and so, here I am still...

I pray that this book may become a sort of "plain-language practical guide" or "field manual" of sorts, in helping the many hurting and wounded soldiers in the army of God to understand a few crucial things and then get healed and delivered of their **spiritual infections**, become strengthened and skilled in the use of the Word and the Sword of the Spirit, take their place in the mighty army that God intended us all to be a part of, and then, even become a major pain in the neck of our adversaries...for a change.

He has also revealed to me prophetically: it is about time that the army of darkness be concerned and even worried about us! We are not to be arrogant, ever...**but we were never, ever, meant to cower in fear of the enemy either.** We are to fear Him (God) only <u>and the devils are supposed to be subject unto us</u> **through His Name** (Luke 10:17).

It is time for us to rise up with our Leader, Who cannot be defeated, for He has already conquered and defeated our adversaries, and now move on to our mission and calling: becoming administrators of His victory and, **through Him, His Name, His Word and His Spirit's power alone**, invade the territories that the enemy armies have illegally occupied and also remove them!! Even as the allied armies took back the countries occupied by Hitler and his armies in WWII, we are to go forth boldly like a mighty Allied army, take back **all** the occupied territories and **forcibly eject the invaders and trespassers from our lives.**

Only a ground invasion effectively removes the enemy. It was necessary in WWII, and in any war that has been or is to be won...and it is also necessary in the war that has been brought upon each of us by the evil trespassers of the army of darkness.

It is time. He ordained it...and it has arrived.

"Let him who has ears to hear, hear what the Spirit is saying..."

INTRODUCTION

I'll get right to the point: this book is about the solution to a big and urgent problem.

The problem is that the Body of Messiah is not what it is supposed to be: a mighty army that is triumphant over the army of darkness.

God's army is largely fighting itself and is largely sick, not just physically, **but perhaps even more so emotionally**. It is also spiritually weak and ineffective. **It is full of division, contention and strife. It does not get along with itself. It is full of broken relationships at all levels. And, it does not love people anywhere near *enough* nor does it seem genuine *or consistent enough.*** It also lacks the power of God that it ought to have and manifest.

God does not lack in love, health or power...but His army today does not have nearly *enough* of His love, health or power.

Until these problems can be overcome, the Body of Christ will continue to be a group that is fragmented, weak, sick **and largely ineffective in what it has been called to be and do. It will continue to fail to** demonstrate to the world *enough* of the love, health and power of an Almighty God.

The problem is that <u>we are not recognizing the real enemy...*enough*</u>.

As much as we think we know about spiritual warfare and the enemy, we **do not yet recognize them *clearly enough*.** And, because of that, we **do not remove them *nearly enough*.**

And **without removing them enough,** they continue to wreak too much havoc, not only on the unbelievers of the world, but also upon the believers, which are supposed to be the people that are able to be triumphant over them. And they wreak this havoc **by <u>sabotaging</u> our love, health, power <u>and holiness</u>.**

But **we can't solve any problem until** we **truly understand what is at the root of it**. So, inevitably, we'll have to talk about **this problem**. In fact, we're going to **dissect** many aspects of this problem.

If anyone says *"don't talk so much about the problem"* or *"don't give this so much importance"*, I respond with the old saying *"we can't fix it if we don't know where it's broken"*. **We cannot conquer or defeat what we do not understand enough**. People are destroyed, and go into captivity, for lack of knowledge (Hosea 4:6, Isaiah 5:13).

So how much understanding of this problem is "enough" or "not enough"? If we are not obtaining desirable results, it is "not enough". If we still have a problem, we do not (yet) have enough knowledge or understanding about the problem. *Something* is missing. *The solution* is missing.

I guarantee you: this book is **not** about "pointing a finger" to anyone in any situation. It's **not** just for the sake of talking nonsense, **nor** is it a rhetorical or intellectual exercise. **It's about understanding situations and recognizing *the real culprits of our problems*, in order to move as soon as possible to solving them**...so that the people can be restored and made whole. It is to **remove "darkness"** and **"sinfulness"** from our lives and **bring the Light and "holiness" more fully** into the place where "holiness" has the real dominion of our lives.

Having said that right up front, let me now tell you more about the purpose of this book: **solving a big and urgent problem.**

Who is "our enemy"? Collectively, it is the army of darkness...*whatever that is.* Many say it is a particular spiritual being. But more accurately, it is that person **and the large army that he leads.** But sadly, though many are offended at the mere suggestion, we are largely not recognizing them when we encounter them. I know that I myself did not recognize them all that well until a time not too long ago.

Here's an analogy or a "parable": just like Hitler led an army of Nazis, our enemy leads an army of many members of the "army of darkness". Most allied soldiers in WWII did not fight Hitler himself. But they sure fought, in bloody combat, members of his army, under his leadership, which agreed with his ideologies. Likewise, most of us may never encounter "the enemy himself"...but we sure do battle **many members of his army**, who are bent on the same objective as their leader: to steal, kill and destroy (John 10:10).

So, *they* keep hanging around, unnoticed, undetected, sabotaging us day after day, and all the while, we are fighting flesh and blood people that we see one-dimensionally as "wicked people", even though we are told that we do not wrestle flesh and blood but rather, *spiritual* wickedness.

Sadly, we see parents, children, spouses, and brethren in our congregations, even pastors and ministers, fighting each other, or their sheep, with all manner of malice, suspicion and inner conflict. Are we not supposed to love, forgive, release, pardon, think the best, and forbear? We know that we are supposed to.

But somehow, we can't seem to do what we know we are supposed to, or even want to, do (Romans 7:17-20). It seems that we do not have an effective enough solution to the **"sin in the flesh"** or the **"sinful nature" problems**.

Perhaps we do not understand enough about those problems either. (The **second chapter** of this book analyzes this problem in detail, and is **key** for the solution.)

The good news is that God Almighty has ordained and set an appointed time to pour out upon His people **the understanding and discernment necessary** to **recognize and identify the enemy completely**. He has also begun to give His people **His plan and strategy** to then **move on to removing and eradicating** the spiritual enemies, first from ourselves, and then to humbly but effectively help others remove them from their midst and from wherever we might encounter them.

It is not that God did not provide what was necessary for the job. It is that **the enemy is a deceiver and is, along with his army, <u>largely hidden and concealed</u>** *<u>even until now</u>*.

But God is and has always been in control of all things. He has "factored in" all of the choices of His created beings, both seen and unseen, and the time has finally come when He is revealing to us, by His Spirit, the things we need to see and understand <u>so we can fully exercise His authority on earth</u> as it is in heaven.

And we will now be able to take authority over the powers of darkness like we are supposed to and like we have never done before.

It is already happening.

This book is written with the express purpose of **exposing the enemy and his army's presence and devices in a clear, simple and accurate manner**. It will expose them in various situations and point out the ways in which not recognizing the enemy hurts and sabotages us.

By doing this, we are led to the solution to this problem: <u>effectively removing them</u>.

The time has arrived when the people of God will be able to, more effectively than ever, **<u>rise up</u>** and follow in the purpose of Jesus: ...***For this purpose the Son of God was manifested, that he might destroy the works of the devil*** (1 John 3: 8).

Read on for **the solution** to this **serious and urgent problem**...

Special Note on the Names of God

As a **Believer** that embraces the Hebraic roots and the continuity of our faith, I am aware that most "Christians" and "Messianics" might use different names for our God and that many issues often arise out of this.

I have truly thought long and hard about how to present the names of the Holy One of Israel in this book. If I were to use only "Christian names", some "Messianics" might fault any such use. If I were to use only Hebraic or "Messianic names", some "Christians" may be "turned off" or simply confused initially by the "different names".

Greatly desiring to give offense to no one, yet understanding that I cannot completely please everyone, I settled on "a partial transition".

Since most of us begin our walk of faith using the "Christian names", I begin this book using them to refer to our God. As the book progresses, beginning on Chapter 7, I make the transition to *mostly* using the Hebraic names.

Again, I am aware of the many debates and opinions regarding the names of our Deity and the many aspects involved. For the record, I am not of the opinion that the way we use the names of God is a salvation issue. Therefore, I choose not to have division over this topic.

I am personally persuaded that He Who saved me by faith did so long before I learned more about Him. Having said that, as I progressed in the knowledge of

Him and in relationship with Him, I feel I have been led to transition "back" towards the restoration of many Hebraic aspects that I now realize never really "went out of style" or "passed away".

My prayer is that we simply allow each man and woman to be fully persuaded in his or her own mind and heart, knowing of Whom they have learned these things, while we love, forbear and forgive one another for any errors or differences we may have "along the way" to the Millennial Kingdom and the New Jerusalem.

Nevertheless, for those that may simply *prefer* a version of this book that *exclusively* uses either Christian or Hebraic names, please feel free to contact me at the email address at the end of the book, as plans for such versions may be in the works.

1

"FOR WE WRESTLE NOT AGAINST FLESH AND BLOOD..."

The first step in "recognizing the real enemy" is to zero in on some key aspects of the enemy.

Ephesians 6:12 is a very familiar Scripture that contains a key aspect about the enemy and starts with who the enemy **is not** before telling us who the enemy **really is**:

> **Ephesians 6:12 For we wrestle not against flesh and blood, but against principalities, against powers, against the rulers of the darkness of this world, against spiritual wickedness in high [places].**

What this verse tells us is that we do not wrestle against flesh-and-blood, meaning, we do not battle "human beings". Scripture tells us that we are **not wrestling people** themselves. Instead, it tells us that we are wrestling with **spirits,** such as "rulers" of darkness and "wickedness" that is "spiritual" in nature.

Another familiar and important Scripture about our "spiritual battle" is in 2 Corinthians 10:4 and 5:

> **2 Corinthians 10:4 (For the weapons of our warfare [are] not carnal, but mighty through God to the pulling down of strong holds;)**
> **5 Casting down imaginations, and every high thing that exalteth itself against the knowledge of God, and bringing into captivity every thought to the obedience of Christ;**

So, if the weapons of our warfare are <u>not carnal</u>, or physical, then our weapons are **spiritual**. This goes along perfectly with Ephesians 6:12. These two Scriptures give us the following:

1. We do not battle human beings; **we battle spirits** that are **wicked**.
2. Our **weapons** are not physical or carnal but rather **spiritual**.

These two Scriptures and principles may be common and seem like nothing new to the reader. <u>But yet, many believers are still fighting with human beings and fighting with physical or carnal weapons</u>. Let us look closer at what we may not be realizing from these Scriptures and how these issues play out in our physical lives.

Do We Battle Physical or Spiritual Enemies?

The answer is **both**, depending on how we look at it. But at the root of the physical enemies is always a **spiritual** enemy.

For example, if the spiritual enemy of say, anger, attacks you, what would that attack be like? It would probably be something like <u>thoughts and/or feelings of</u>

anger would flood you about, say, the neighbor whose dog barks, or about the guy in church who parked in your parking spot, or takes your usual place to sit. Or, cuts in front of you at the cafeteria and takes the last piece of pie that you wanted. That would be the spiritual enemy attacking you.

But, what if you got so angry when those things happened that you went ahead and actually acted out of that anger and went and punched the guy? Then **you became the physical enemy** of that guy.

Let's examine what happened. The spiritual enemy came to you and gave you his feelings of anger and gave you "reasons" for that anger in your thoughts. It may have sounded like "that jerk did it again! I can't believe he took my parking spot/seat/pie!" You then got carried away with "your" anger and the reasons for it and "how wrong it was", so you went ahead and punched the guy for it.

Well, two things happened. The spiritual enemy gave you his thoughts and feelings and you then agreed with it all and went along with it, and maybe other thoughts and impulses, like "I'm not going to let him get away with that! I'm going to show him!" And, once you agreed with and went along with that spiritual enemy, you became the <u>physical</u> counterpart of that <u>spiritual</u> enemy against the other person.

What we need to realize out of this example is what happens in just about every other situation. The pattern is the same. A **spiritual enemy**, of some sort, attacks us and gives us **his** thoughts and feelings. They may be thoughts and feelings of **anger** or of **worry**, **fear** or **anxiety**. Or they could be of **sadness**, **loneliness** or **depression**. Or they could be of feeling

unlovable, **inferior**, **unworthy**, or **rejected** and **despised** or of feeling **bitter**, **resentful, hateful** or **critical** and **accusatory** towards someone.

One thing that we as believers must realize in **all** the above possible situations is this: those thoughts and feelings do not come "out of thin air". Another thing is that they do not come "**only** from you". They **may** come from you alright. But, **before they were** "**your**" thoughts and feelings, **where** did you **first get them from**? Did they come from God?

"*Of course not*", is what most of you would answer.

"My" Thoughts and Feelings: Mine or the Enemy's *Through Me*?

Most of the believers I've discussed this with often answer me that those negative thoughts and feelings named above are certainly not coming from God. But when I ask them where they come from, the surprising majority of them tell me that they come "from me". They then tell me how it is their "sinful nature" or that they have had those thoughts and feelings of anger or fear or anxiety or depression or sadness or unworthiness for a long time. They might even tell me that their parents or grandparents "have always been that way".

What I would emphasize at this point is that when I ask those same people where their **holy** thoughts and feelings, such as **love, joy, peace, patience** and **forgiveness**, come from, they are all quick to say "from God!" And indeed they are from God. **Initially they come from God, and then they become ours**. We

agree with and **receive** those thoughts and feelings and we go ahead and **act them out**. And we hopefully learn to think and be that way all the time.

It is the same with **un-holy** thoughts or feelings: **before** they were "ours", they came **from the enemy or his army**. The devil is the father of lies and a murderer from the beginning (John 8:44) and iniquity was found in him (Ezekiel 28:15) and they then entered into the world by one man (Romans 5:12) in the Garden of Eden. Notice that they **existed before** Adam's disobedience and simply **entered by, but were not created by**, Adam's disobedience.

So, if our **holy** thoughts and feelings come from the **Holy** Spirit...then why wouldn't our **un-holy** thoughts and feelings also come from <u>an</u> **un-holy** spirit...of some sort? I will submit to you the reason right now and prove it out later throughout this book:

> *<u>God has not desired to conceal from us</u> that our holiness comes from Him. <u>However, the enemy, the deceiver, the accuser of the brethren, <u>absolutely has desired</u>, and been successful to a great extent, <u>to conceal from us that all of our un-holiness first comes and originates from him and his army of un-holy spirits</u>!*

It has often been said that thoughts come from one of three sources: God, the enemy or from ourselves. That is true. However, we must realize that **our thoughts** will **either** be <u>in agreement with the thoughts of God</u>, as we become transformed by the renewing of our mind with the Word of God, **or** our thoughts will be <u>in agreement with</u> and be conformed to the world and the "god of this world". There really is no middle ground.

We must realize that man does not **originate** anything. There is nothing new under the sun. God created everything and is the only Creator. He created all things and all living beings, **whether unseen or seen, spiritual or physical**. And all those beings were given **the freedom to choose to obey or disobey God**. Adam and Eve had that ability and so do you and I. What we must remember is that the enemy of our souls, your adversary, the devil (1 Peter 5:8) also was given that ability to choose and he chose to rebel and disobey God. And ever since, he has been the enemy of God and has worked against God's creation and mankind. He competes with God to coax us **into following him** instead of God.

Radio God or Radio Devil? – It Started at the Garden of Eden

The fact that the Holy One is ever speaking to us and seeking to "coach us" into *holy* thoughts and feelings and acts, all the while the *un-holy* one and his army are **also** ever speaking to us and seeking to "coach us" into all manner of un-holy thoughts and feelings and acts, is what I've come to refer to as man **either** listening to "Radio God" **or** "Radio Devil". This fact can be seen since the beginning in the Garden of Eden. Even back then, **Adam and Eve were "not alone" with God.**

> **Genesis 3:1 Now the serpent was more subtil than any beast of the field which the LORD God had made. And he said unto the woman, Yea, hath**

God said, Ye shall not eat of every tree of the garden?

2 And the woman said unto the serpent, We may eat of the fruit of the trees of the garden:

3 But of the fruit of the tree which [is] in the midst of the garden, God hath said, Ye shall not eat of it, neither shall ye touch it, lest ye die.

4 And the serpent said unto the woman, Ye shall not surely die:

5 For God doth know that in the day ye eat thereof, then your eyes shall be opened, and ye shall be as gods, knowing good and evil.

6 And when the woman saw that the tree [was] good for food, and that it [was] pleasant to the eyes, and a tree to be desired to make [one] wise, she took of the fruit thereof, and did eat, and gave also unto her husband with her; and he did eat.

7 And the eyes of them both were opened, and they knew that they [were] naked; and they sewed fig leaves together, and made themselves aprons.

8 And they heard the voice of the LORD God walking in the garden in the cool of the day: and Adam and his wife hid themselves from the presence of the LORD God amongst the trees of the garden.

9 And the LORD God called unto Adam, and said unto him, Where [art] thou?

10 And he said, I heard thy voice in the garden, and I was afraid, because I [was] naked; and I hid myself.

11 And he said, Who told thee that thou [wast] naked? Hast thou eaten of the tree, whereof I commanded thee that thou shouldest not eat?

There are **two things** that are worth noting carefully in this familiar but important passage of Scripture. One is that in verse 1, we see that serpent (the devil) *questioning* what God has said ("...*Yea, hath God said?...*") *and seeking to cause doubt as* *to why* and to His motives, which he then elaborates on and accuses God of just wanting to withhold something back from the man and the woman. Also worth noting is that in verse 11, responding to Adam, God asks: "*Who told you* that you wast naked?" What we may not have realized before is that **someone did tell Adam** that he was naked!

Before this episode, there was no fear in them and no shame of their nakedness. But, immediately after their disobedience, **something** told him that he was naked. I submit to you that **"things"** <u>do not talk or tell anything</u>. Therefore, it had to be a "*someone*" that told Adam that he was naked. He also said he was afraid! So, he also felt <u>fear</u> "<u>because</u> he was naked".

According to Adam's response in verse 10, he **felt** afraid **because** he was naked. And from God's response, we see that some**one** **told** him he was naked. So, do we not see that <u>it was not God that told him that</u>? Do we not realize that **some other being** gave Adam the thoughts and feelings that he was naked and that therefore he had and felt that fear?

Ever Since the Garden: Either God's Voice or The Enemy's

So, we see from the above that, since the beginning of human man and woman's presence in this world, the enemy and his kingdom were already here on earth after falling from heaven (Isaiah 14:12, Luke 10:18). They were just **waiting to "gain access"**.

When Adam and Eve disobeyed God, suddenly **"negative emotions"** such as **fear**, **shame**, **blame** and **accusation** were manifested in Adam and Eve. The Bible calls these "negative emotions" **sin**:

> **Romans 5:12 Wherefore, as by one man _sin_ _entered into the world_, and death by sin; and so death passed upon all men, for that all have sinned:**

Notice that Scripture says that sin **entered**: it did not "originate" nor was "birthed". "Original sin" did <u>not</u> originate in Adam. It was first found in Lucifer:

> **Ezekiel 28:15 Thou [wast] perfect in thy ways from the day that thou wast created, _till iniquity was found in thee_.**

It was _that sin_ which entered through Adam's disobedience. Yes, Adam did sin...**when he disobeyed**. Until that point, Adam did not have sin. The enemy had sin and iniquity and had been cast down. But it was not until Adam yielded himself **to the sinful spirit of the enemy** that he "became one" with it. This is made plain by Romans 6:16:

> **Romans 6:16 Know ye not, that _to whom ye yield yourselves servants to obey, his servants ye are to whom ye obey; whether of sin_ unto death, or of obedience unto righteousness?**

See? Once he yielded himself and obeyed the enemy, only then did Adam become a servant to sin. And as stated above in Romans 5:12, that's when sin entered into the world.

So, we see that **what entered** is not just a "what" but rather **a whole kingdom of sinful, rebellious beings,** all under the leadership of Satan himself! And yes, with that came a separation from God (spiritual death) that could only be remedied by the last Adam (Jesus).

Not only did beings that had the "characteristics" and "attributes" **of fear, shame, guilt, accusation and blame enter in,** but so did every other "negative emotion" and "negative thought" that is not present in God the Father, the Son or the Holy Spirit. Everything un-godly and un-holy that there is, which belongs to the kingdom of darkness, entered into man and quickly spoiled God's creation. So quickly in fact, that by Genesis Chapter 6, God observed that the thoughts of man's heart were to do evil continually and it became so bad that God repented of having made man and decided to destroy them all.

Realize that between Genesis Chapter 3 and Chapter 6, that was what happened! It was **not "man" in and of himself!** It was the "sin"-ful **beings, living and EVIL beings that entered into man and their world,** which quickly spoiled their hearts and brought them the thoughts to do evil continually! Do you see **what really happened to us**? But, it was not "us"! It was **"them". They** (the sinful beings that Adam went along with and entered into our world dimension) that **have been "messing with us" ever since!**

That is "the real enemy"!

Ever since, Satan and his kingdom of darkness have been influencing mankind into speaking and acting out his thoughts and objectives. Some examples are below:

- Peter seeks to dissuade Jesus from going to the Cross (Matthew 16:22-23).

- Judas decides to betray Jesus (Luke 22:3; John 13:2, 27).
- Ananias and Sapphira lie and keep back money (Acts 5:3-4, 9).
- The fear and timidity in Timothy was from a spirit of fear (2 Timothy 1:7).
- Elymas the sorcerer who withstood Paul and Barnabas at Paphos (Acts 13:8-11).
- The girl with the spirit of divination (Acts 16:16).

Only Living Beings Have Thoughts, Feelings or Desires

Now we come back to something we stated earlier: that thoughts do not come "out of thin air". **Thoughts can only come from a mind** and dead things do not have a mind and do not think. **Dead things also do not feel nor have feelings to give**. So, we agree that only "living beings" can feel or have feelings and that only "intelligent beings" can have thoughts in their minds. **Without a mind, there are no thoughts** that can be had.

These assertions may seem obvious but it is important that these things be made clear. Why? Because we need to realize clearly that thoughts and feelings can only come from a living being. They cannot exist outside of, or independent or apart from, some **living being** with a mind and the ability to feel feelings.

This allows us to realize that if we experience any thoughts or feelings, or hear any voices within ourselves or in our minds, or that we have any "urges", **we are being contacted or influenced by a living**

being of some sort. And, we then have to ask ourselves: **_who_** is talking to us and/or **whose** thoughts are we receiving or **whose** feelings are we feeling or even "**whose** urges" are we sensing?

From the previous examination of the first Scriptural episode of Godly vs. ungodly influence, we now submit that **all Godly thoughts and feelings come from God** and **all un-godly thoughts and feelings come from the enemy and his army**.

Again, **that** is the "real enemy": **the devil and his kingdom of evil spirits!**

Does This Mean We Just "Blame the Enemy"?

Absolutely not. What this actually does is **increase our responsibility** to "deal with the enemy". But being able to identify the enemy and "separate them from ourselves" does help *immensely and is crucial*. That will be explained further in the next chapters.

We now realize that "**we** are **not the problem**". We may have "problem beings" to deal with but **they are the problem**, not us. There is a difference! And as you will see, this difference makes a **significant** difference. Believe me, **our enemy does not want us to know this and does not want you to know this!**

For now, we see that we as human beings have always been placed in the position of choosing to obey God or disobeying God.

> **Deuteronomy 30:19** I call heaven and earth to record this day against you, [that] I have set before you <u>life and death, blessing and cursing: therefore choose life,</u> that both thou and thy seed may live:
> **20** That thou mayest love the LORD thy God, [and] that thou mayest <u>obey his voice,</u> and that thou mayest cleave unto him: for he [is] thy life, and the length of thy days: that thou mayest dwell in the land which the LORD sware unto thy fathers, to Abraham, to Isaac, and to Jacob, to give them.

We can now realize more clearly that if we disobey the Word of God in any area, we are being **led in that direction by the enemy of God, our adversary, and his kingdom of evil spirits.** How can we know this? We know **because <u>God would never lead us into disobedience to His Word</u>**. And since dead beings cannot give us ungodly feelings or thoughts or reasons that would lead against God's Word, we can conclude that **<u>those beings must be on the enemy's side</u>**.

In the next chapter, we will look closer at "sin" and at the concept of "the flesh" so as to continue to clarify how it is exactly that we can recognize and then conclusively defeat the enemy among us.

2

WHAT ABOUT "SIN" AND "THE FLESH"?

In the first chapter, we looked at the fact that only living beings can have thoughts or feelings. We also established that the enemy of God and His people is Satan and his kingdom of darkness. They are evil spirits that seek to guide us into rebellion and disobedience to God and His Word. They first did this in the Garden of Eden and deceived Adam and Eve into disobeying, at which point they all "entered into the world" (Romans 5:12) and have been influencing man ever since with every wicked and evil thought, emotion, nature and act ever known.

Therefore, we are learning to recognize that we are ever having to **choose** to follow God's influence through the **thoughts, feelings and desires of the Holy Spirit** within us **or** the **thoughts, feelings and desires of the enemy and his evil spirits**. There is no "middle ground".

However, much has been said about "the flesh" and man's "fallen nature" or "sinful nature". In this chapter, we will look more closely at these phrases and will see that we are still either controlled by God's Holy Spirit or by other un-holy spirits. In fact, we will see that <u>the enemy has been masterfully concealing himself and his kingdom</u> **through these phrases and "concepts"**!

As we recognize that Scripture does teach us clearly about the relationship between the flesh and what "sin" really is, we will be able to *differentiate* **between the enemy and between ourselves,** which is the very thing that is going to allow us to be more discerning than ever and will be the key for us to also be more victorious over the kingdom and powers of darkness than ever. Keep reading!

But...Aren't "We" the Problem?

We already looked at the original problem in the Garden of Eden. We must realize that the problem was **not with man's nature** in the way that he was made by God. The problem in the garden was **not man's "sinful nature".** The problem was **that a sinful being and his army deceived, coaxed and coached man into disobeying God! And, when man disobeyed, *they* entered into the world!**

> **Romans 5:12 Wherefore, as by one man sin entered into the world, and death by sin; and so death passed upon all men, for that all have sinned:**

Do you see? Adam did <u>not</u> become contaminated with some <u>chemical or biological</u> impurity. <u>Neither</u> did he become a "defective creation" because of any "<u>psychological</u> condition". What he became "infected with" was a *spiritual* "impurity"! <u>Impure spirit beings</u> – Satan and his army – <u>entered</u> man. **They** entered man! See the difference and the separation between *them* and **man**?

That fact alone is something the enemy does not want us to be clear about. He much rather <u>wants us believing the lie that "we became defective" in some inherent, integral way</u>. Because he then adds the lie that "such an inherent condition <u>locks us into helplessly being sinful beings forever with no hope of being holy</u>".

But if that was so, then why does God tell us to be holy? Why does Scripture ask us so often to sanctify and cleanse ourselves if these things were not possible?

Many believers do admit it is possible...but this lie, even when it is not completely believed, still deceives believers into **thinking that we must accept**, "make allowances" or "make accommodations" or "make room for" some **sins** in our walk. They <u>believe that "we will never be sinless"</u>. *All that does is make us "try less hard" and strive less for holiness*. That may be the most devastating effect of this lie. To one degree or another, it deceives the believer into thinking that we cannot escape having some sins. But the Word of God exhorts us repeatedly to cleanse ourselves from <u>all</u> filthiness of the flesh and spirit and to perfect our holiness!

2 Corinthians 7:1 Having therefore these promises, dearly beloved, <u>let us cleanse ourselves from all filthiness of the flesh and spirit, perfecting holiness</u> in the fear of God.

And, what promises does He refer to? The previous verses show us:

> **2 Corinthians 6:16 And <u>what agreement hath the temple of God with idols? for ye are the temple of the living God</u>; as God hath said, I will dwell in them, and walk in [them]; and I will be their God, and they shall be my people.**
> **17 Wherefore come out from among them, and <u>be ye separate</u>, saith the Lord, and <u>touch not the unclean</u> [thing]; and I will receive you,**
> **18 And will be a Father unto you, and ye shall be my sons and daughters, saith the Lord Almighty.**

God is telling us and commanding us (not suggesting) to not have any agreement with what is unholy and to separate ourselves from the unholy and the unclean. Why would He ask and command such things if such were not completely possible?

The good news is that through Jesus the Messiah/Yeshua HaMashiach, <u>we can regain our "spiritual purity"</u>! What happened in the Garden of Eden can be reversed. We can "go back" to spiritual purity. And that re-connects us to the fellowship with God that was lost in the garden. That is what "going back to Eden" really means. Hallelujah!

So, What About Sin and the Flesh?

Let us now look at the concepts of "sin" and "the flesh" so we can understand that the truths stated so far really are in the Scriptures but that they have been "explained" in a way that is simply not true. **The enemy has truly "clouded" the issue of "sin" and "the flesh"**. It will be evident in the rest of this chapter and also in Chapter 5.

The Book of Romans contains a great treatise on sin. However, some of the key issues about sin and the flesh have been "tampered with" in order to keep man deceived about the facts and the truth, which, in turn, hide the simple solution to the real problem and culprit, which is the presence of the enemy's evil spirits.

Romans 7 contains some crucial truths in verses 17 through 20.

> **Romans 7:17 Now then it is no more I that do it, but sin that <u>dwelleth</u> in me.**
> **18 For I know that in me (that is, in my flesh,) <u>dwelleth</u> no good thing: for to will is present with me; but [how] to perform that which is good I find not.**
> **19 For the good that I would I do not: but the evil which I would not, that I do.**
> **20 Now if I do that I would not, it is <u>no more I that do it, but sin</u> that <u>dwelleth</u> in me.**

Notice that Scripture says that "<u>the doer</u>" of the sin <u>is the sin that **dwells**</u>. We must not overlook these words. Three times alone is this word used here. I believe every Word of God is deliberate, meaningful and purposeful, not "accidental" nor "of no consequence".

> **2 Timothy 3:16 All scripture [is] given by inspiration of God, and [is] profitable for doctrine, for reproof, for correction, for instruction in righteousness:**
> **17 That the man of God may be perfect, throughly furnished unto all good works.**

Therefore, we must form our doctrines based on what the Word truly says and it must not ever go against any part of the Scripture.

In Romans 7, verses 17 through 20, Scripture chooses an interesting word for the sin and that word is "**dwells**". We must realize that Paul is explaining in verses 17 and 20 that there is **a difference** and **a separation** between him *and* the one that does the sin. He is also saying that "it" dwells, meaning that "it" is "alive". He also specifies in verse 18 that "it" dwells!

Do you see? If sin is an object or a thing, it would not "dwell" or "reside" or "live" in the flesh. It might "sit" or "be located" in the flesh but it would not "*dwell*".

Also, Paul says that it is the sin that **does** what he does not want to do. He says plainly that it is **not him that does the sin** but that it is the **sin** "itself" that **does** the sin.

Do you now see why we took the time in Chapter 1 to make the seemingly obvious point that "things do not think or feel" nor are alive? Things can't do anything and things certainly don't "act up" or "act" out any acts. **Only living beings can "act"**.

Therefore, Paul is clearly telling us that:

- Sin **dwells** or lives; **it is alive;**
- Sin **does** sin; sin **actually does** what he does not want to do
- Sin dwells **in** the flesh;
- Sin is **separate from** the flesh; and
- Sin is **not the same as** "the flesh".

Do you see? Understanding what Scripture plainly tells us, and not what we have been taught to understand, is the way that the man of God may be perfect and thoroughly furnished unto all good works.

By now, you may be hearing, thinking or remembering that "this is not what it means". Well then, let us continue to see what the Word tells us about what "dwells in the flesh".

What Dwells in the Flesh?

The Master Himself said:

> **Luke 11:24 When the <u>unclean spirit</u> is gone out of a man, <u>he</u> walketh through dry places, seeking rest; and finding none, <u>he</u> saith, <u>I will</u> return unto my house whence I came out.**
> **25 And when he cometh, he findeth [it] swept and garnished.**
> **26 Then goeth he, and taketh [to him] seven other spirits more wicked than himself; and they enter in, and <u>dwell</u> there: and the last [state] of that man is worse than the first.**

Did you see? He says that "**an unclean spirit**" can go **out of** a man (!) and then even seeks to return with seven other spirits more wicked than himself (!!) and **they enter in that man** and <u>dwell</u> there! Do you see it? Do you read it? Do you believe it? <u>Or do you "rationalize it away"</u>? Have you been taught that "this can't be"? Why not? Whatever "reason" you may have, it contradicts Scripture and the Master's own Word.

Now, in case you may have been taught or told that the above passage in Luke "*does not apply to a born-again believer"* or *"is only for the unsaved"*, for now, please realize that the passage has no such condition, qualifier or statement even remotely made. Nor is there any such support or statement in Scripture. Thus, it applies to any "man". (More on this topic in this chapter and the rest of this book, but particularly in Chapters 5 and 7.)

Further, do you see that there is "another spirit" that is "another being" in this situation **in addition to the man**?

This illustrates that:

- there is such a thing as an "unclean spirit".
- those spirits are "another person" or "another entity".
- that entity:
  - travels and goes places,
  - **talks**,
  - **thinks**,
  - has **"its" own will**, and
  - even **decides** to do things.
- those spirits can **go "get others"**.
- spirits **can enter** into a man and **dwell** there.

Are these things not shocking? They may be shocking but they are true and they are the Truth of God's Word (John 17:17).

Let's look at another passage of Scripture that teaches about the interaction between unclean spirits and mankind and the effects of these spirits upon mankind. Mark 5:1 and Luke 8:26 tell of the encounter Jesus had with a man who had "many devils" afflicting him. From these verses we find the following adverse effects upon that poor man. He:

- wore no clothes;
- abode not in any house, but rather in the tombs and in the mountains;
- cut himself with stones;
- cried;
- was often chained with chains and fetters;
- would pluck the chains asunder and break the fetters in pieces; and
- no one could tame him.

Now this was one afflicted man! Today, doctors and psychologists would likely label him insane, violent, and incurable, seek to restrain and bind him and probably prescribe medications (drugs) to control his behavior! <u>But Jesus dealt with the spirits</u> *causing the behavior* instead!

What is also worth noting is what the verses concluding the account tell us.

> **Luke 8:35 Then they went out to see what was done; and came to Jesus, and found the man, <u>out of whom the devils were departed</u>, sitting at the feet of Jesus, <u>clothed, and in his right mind</u>: and they were afraid.**

We see that the devils were departed out of that man, making it clear that the devils had been **inside** that man. We also see that, once the spirits were departed out, the man was **clothed <u>and</u> in his right mind**.

That's the kind of difference it can make when we get "these other spirits" out of us! Blessed be the Name of the Lord for sending Jesus to do these things for us!

Back to Ephesians 6:12

Remember the verse we looked at in Chapter 1? Are we not seeing further the truth of that verse?

> **Ephesians 6:12: For we wrestle not against flesh and blood, but against principalities, against powers, against the rulers of the darkness of this world, against spiritual wickedness in high [places].**

Let us look at another example in Scripture in which Paul perfectly displays this "separation" or difference between mankind and the evil spirits that can dwell in man, that commit sins and that we wrestle with.

> **Acts 16:16 And it came to pass, as we went to prayer, a certain damsel possessed with a spirit of divination met us, which brought her masters much gain by soothsaying:**
> **17 The same followed Paul and us, and cried, saying, These men are the servants of the most high God, which shew unto us the way of salvation.**
> **18 And this did she many days. But Paul, being grieved, turned and said to the spirit, I command thee in the name of Jesus Christ to come out of her. And he came out the same hour.**

Again, we see that there was "another spirit" in her, separate from her, which was not her. And in this case, this "other spirit being" caused her to speak divinations, even "godly sounding", and things which did not come from God!

And in this case, Paul perfectly demonstrated the very thing he tells us in Ephesians 6:12. He wrestled and dealt with the spirit in the girl and not the girl herself. **He did not grab the "physical girl" by the neck**, for example. He dealt with, and cast out, the spirit that was in the girl. Do you see?

Back to "Radio God" or "Radio Devil"

Remember how we said in Chapter 1 that we are either listening to the voice, thoughts and feelings of God or the thoughts, feelings and influences of the enemy? Perhaps the best example of this in the Word of God can be seen through the very apostle Peter in Matthew Chapter 16:

> **Matthew 16:15 He saith unto them, But whom say ye that I am?**
> **16 And Simon Peter answered and said, Thou art the Christ, the Son of the living God.**
> **17 And Jesus answered and said unto him, Blessed art thou, Simon Barjona: for flesh and blood hath not revealed [it] unto thee, but my Father which is in heaven.**

Here we see that Peter heard "Radio God" and had received from God the Father, Who is a Spirit and not flesh and blood (John 4:24). God gave him that **thought**. And that thought was Truth from God.

However, just a few verses later, we see that *Peter also heard and received and agreed with another thought from another living being:*

> Matthew 16:21 From that time forth began Jesus to shew unto his disciples, how that he must go unto Jerusalem, and suffer many things of the elders and chief priests and scribes, and be killed, and be raised again the third day.
> 22 Then Peter took him, and began to rebuke him, saying, Be it far from thee, Lord: this shall not be unto thee.
> 23 But he turned, and said unto Peter, Get thee behind me, Satan: thou art an offence unto me: for thou savourest not the things that be of God, but those that be of men.

Do you see? In this case, **it was Satan who had made Peter think** that what Jesus said "should not be". Not only did Jesus **identify and recognize whose thought** Peter had heard, agreed with and spoken out, He also shows us "why it sounded good and was accepted by" Peter: he was savoring the things of man above the things which were from God, which Jesus was showing unto His disciples in verse 21. Peter did not discern that those things were from God and instead thought that the "God thing" would be to save Jesus from the sufferings.

In this second instance, Peter heard, **and agreed with**, the deception of "Radio devil".

And So...

In this second chapter, we have examined what sin really is according to Scripture. It is **alive**, it **dwells**, it **does** sin (**acts** of disobedience to God's holiness and commands, desires and objectives). Therefore, we see that "it" is not exactly an "it" at all. It is alive. It lives. It is in fact a kingdom of living spirit beings and they are the ones that are "evil in nature". They are separate from us in being.

However, it is **"they in us"**, that is, in "our flesh", that cause us to suffer evil effects and torments. They give us their thoughts, even words and deeds. They cause us to think and act according to them and often don't even realize it, as seen in the apostle Peter!

If we "become one with them" and they indwell us, and/or give us their thoughts and objectives, and we go along with them, agree with them and act out their desires, **their** evil nature becomes ours also.

> **Romans 6:16 Know ye not, that <u>to whom ye yield yourselves servants to obey, his servants ye are</u> to whom ye obey; <u>whether of sin</u> unto death, or of obedience unto righteousness?**

Do you see that in the above verse, to whom we yield ourselves, we become their servants? We must not yield ourselves to these beings!

Judas Iscariot did so and look at what happened to him. **First, Satan put it into his heart** to betray Jesus:

> **John 13:2 And supper being ended, <u>the devil having now put into the heart of Judas Iscariot</u>, Simon's [son], to betray him;**

And then, he outright enters into Judas:

> **John 13:26 Jesus answered, He it is, to whom I shall give a sop, when I have dipped [it]. And when he had dipped the sop, he gave [it] to Judas Iscariot, [the son] of Simon.**

27 And after the sop <u>Satan entered into him</u>. Then said Jesus unto him, That thou doest, do quickly.

Having yielded himself, he became a servant, <u>not to a chemical, biological, psychological or otherwise "non-alive" defect or concept</u>, but rather, **to a living "sin"**, as seen from Romans 6:16.

Therefore, we must realize that "sin" can mean "the act"...but Scripturally, it refers to the sin that entered in the garden through the offense of one man (Romans 5:12) and to whom we can yield ourselves as servants (Romans 6:16) and which dwells in the flesh and that <u>does the sin</u> that Paul did not want to do (Romans 7:17-20).

We also saw that these "things" that dwell in the flesh or inside a man are other spirits, other entities, sinful in nature, that work against God's purposes and harm mankind (Luke 11:24-26; Mark 5:1-19; Luke 8:26-39; Ephesians 6:12; Acts 16:16-19; Matthew 16:21-23; John 13:2, 26-27).

And, in addition to seeing how these evil spirits hinder, afflict and oppose mankind and God, <u>we also see the solution to the problem: Yeshua HaMashiach, the Son of the Living God</u>. He was manifested to destroy the works of the devil and **He cast out devils when He encountered them**.

We must remember that Jesus gave us His Name, authority and commandment to cast out devils as well as heal.

**Luke 10:17 And the seventy returned again with joy, saying, Lord, even the devils are subject unto us through thy name.
18 And he said unto them, I beheld Satan as lightning fall from heaven.
19 Behold, I give unto you power to tread on serpents and scorpions, and over all the power of the enemy: and nothing shall by any means hurt you.**

Matthew 10:8 Heal the sick, cleanse the lepers, raise the dead, cast out devils: freely ye have received, freely give.

This is why **we also must recognize and identify the enemy when the enemy is encountered**: so that "the Solution" can be applied. If Jesus and Paul had not recognized the enemy when they encountered evil spirits in those people, they would not have exercised and applied Jesus' authority and power over the enemies that were afflicting those poor people.

Instead, they might have done like many believers do today: they might call a doctor, a psychologist or a psychiatrist instead! They might prescribe medications, drugs or counseling seeking to "tame" those people and not realize the real issue is that they are being afflicted by devils!

And **that would not deal with the true problem**. It would **only deal with symptoms while the true culprit, the enemy and his evil spirits, would remain "hidden" and "invisible"** to the doctors and psychiatrists!

The spirits would continue to torment and afflict the poor people.

In the next chapter, let us look more closely at what would happen, and how we might be dealing with such instances, if we did not recognize the enemy's work upon people and interpreted problems similar to those above as just "psychological issues".

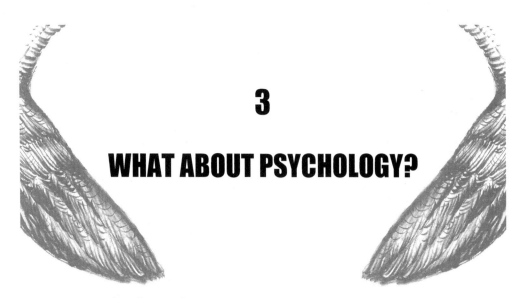

3

WHAT ABOUT PSYCHOLOGY?

In the last chapter, we zeroed in on the fact that man's enemy is not a chemical or biological defect. We identified that the enemy we fight is a kingdom of evil spirits led by Satan. We clarified from Scripture that the enemy and his army existed and were present in the Garden of Eden and were just "waiting for access" to man and this world's physical dimension. And we pointed out that they entered into this world once Adam and Eve disobeyed the commandment of God for them.

We then zeroed in on the fact that Scriptures we may have previously understood to tell us that we have a "sinful nature" or "sin of the flesh" that we can never really control actually teach us that this sin that entered in the garden by one man's offense and disobedience (Romans 5:12) is a group and a kingdom of sinful beings that is alive and does the sins we do not want to do. We also saw several examples in Scripture of the sinful thoughts, feelings and acts that result when these spirits act in and through us.

Seeing that all sin acts come from the activity of, or past teaching of, sin beings and sin spirits, we now begin to realize that this army of spiritual enemies is our real enemy. The people we think we fight against are not the enemy (Ephesians 6:12). And we ourselves are not "defective". What we may have is a spiritual being afflicting us or acting in and through us. The examples in Scripture we looked at showed us how Jesus and Paul dealt with these spiritual enemies affecting people. We closed out the last chapter bringing out that **if we do not recognize** the enemies that Jesus and Paul encountered *as living, evil spirits*, **we would certainly deal with those people very differently from the way they did.**

In this chapter, we will go further in that direction. We will look at what would happen if we think we are encountering "something else". Depending on what we think we are encountering, that determines how we then go about addressing what we think we are encountering. And we will examine whether believers today are perhaps handling these spiritual enemies as if they were "something else". **Tragically, <u>the inevitable consequence of "misdiagnosing the problem" is "mistreating the patient"</u>**.

More specifically, we will look at how these spiritual enemies are being misdiagnosed as <u>"psychological issues"</u> and the less-than-desirable results that come from such a diagnosis.

The Place of Psychology in the Body of Believers Today

Before beginning this discussion, I want to make some **clarifications about what is and is not meant here by "psychology"**. When I speak of "psychology", I mainly refer to **the overall system** of "modern psychology" as the industry that is practiced as a discipline and framework about man's mental and/or emotional **composition and issues**. That also includes its basic views, teachings, foundations and principles, as well as their various methods of "treatment", which are based on its overall views, interpretations and diagnoses. Therefore, **our only goal in reviewing "psychology" is to evaluate whether it is built on God's views...*or not*.**

The concern is simply when it goes against, or ignores, God's information about our "psychological issues". That is all. And, **we do not seek to be "against" the establishment per se**. Actually, we only seek to work **with** the establishment to make it more effective: to make effective what is not effective. And to bring God's light and a true understanding of things anytime there is a "***mis***-understanding".

And so, I am not referring to "our psychology", which would simply refer to our minds: how we all think or process thoughts in our minds. In that sense, we all have "a psychology". It can be said that we all have a "psyche": a mind. But, that would be the mind, emotions and will that God has given us, which is our soul. And **that** is **usually very different from what "secular psychology" is as the system that I described above.**

And, now that I mentioned "secular psychology", I must state that "Christian psychology" can often be a misnomer, as it does not make the whole **system** of doctrine, teachings, foundations and treatments necessarily "compatible" with Bible principles. If a system of teachings, at its root and at its core, is incompatible with and different from the Bible, merely adding or injecting some "Christian principles" into it does not "fix" the non-Christian issues: it merely makes a mixture. And, as stated in Chapter 4, mixing God's ways with other ways is not exactly productive. **It can be ineffective at best or even fatal at worst.**

And so, I will not address "psychology" at length because the very essence of this book is about the fact that **we must have Scriptural solutions to Scriptural problems**. We need **God's spiritual weapons** that are mighty and **not man's weapons that are carnal** (2 Corinthians 10:4). I will only address psychology in order to show why I allege to you that **this is not the solution that our Master and Teacher used and taught**.

The purpose of addressing "psychology" (the system) is simply to contrast how **it** would lead us to diagnose, understand and treat the people and situations that Jesus, Paul and other disciples of the Messiah and children of God dealt with according to Scriptural truths, principles and teachings. In fact, psychology might actually lead us to **mis**-diagnose, **mis**-understand and therefore, **mis**-treat those people and situations.

The foundational Scripture passage for this chapter might be the account of the Gadarene man afflicted by devils in Mark 5:1 and Luke 8:26. This man had some serious problems, and they were mental, emotional and physical. Let us look at them again:

1. He wore no clothes;
2. abode not in any house, but rather in the tombs and in the mountains;
3. cut himself with stones;
4. cried;

5. was often chained with chains and fetters;
6. would pluck the chains asunder and break the fetters in pieces; and
7. no one could tame him.

Now, let's look at how even a "Christian psychologist" might understand and diagnose the above symptoms:

1. Social disorder; lack of learning social norms; mental illness; insanity;
2. isolation; anti-social disorder; dissociative behavior;
3. self-mutilation; self-directed hostility and self-inflicts harm;
4. depression;
5. violent behavior that requires restraint for the good of the patient;
6. difficulty in remaining restrained; displays supernatural strength; possible demonic possession; and
7. no treatment seems to work; insanity; incurable; counseling is ineffective.

While I am not a psychologist or psychiatrist, the above list may not be too far from the way a real psychologist might describe the man in our Scriptural account. They might even add terms of "psychological conditions" such as "bipolar disorder", "schizophrenia" or "manic-depressive".

I would also submit to you that the above **descriptions** also closely resemble the "diagnosis". In other words, they do not really tell us what is really wrong; **they just describe the "emotional" and "psychological" malfunctions**. Then, based on that, psychology has formulated various "treatments" that seek to relieve or modify the observed behavioral symptoms.

In other words, the various "treatments" **do not "cure the fundamental problem"**. They do not "deal with the root" because they do not identify the root. They do not isolate the cause of the problem. And, without identifying the actual cause of the problem, one cannot even know how to correct that cause.

The various treatments might be anything from electro-shock therapy to medicating the patient with various "psycho-active" drugs that alter the behavior by altering the levels of various neurochemicals and other biological substances. The most "effective" ones simply manipulate the levels of these neurochemicals. The "least effective" are just sedatives or stimulants. They are essentially legal and medically-prescribed drugs otherwise known as "downers" or "uppers". They do not "correct" anything. They do not "cure" anything. **And yet they are called "medicines"**.

Why do these "treatments" not really cure anything? Again, it is because they are not formulated to target and fix what is actually causing the malfunction. Yes, they identify what is "too high" or "too low" neurochemically...but they do not know what made that happen in the first place. All they can do is increase or decrease a chemical or give uppers or downers to relieve the exhibited behaviors. This is nothing short of a legal administration of non-medicinal drugs. All they do is "dope up" or "dope down" the person.

All the while, the poor person continues to suffer the thoughts and emotions and actions that we have already seen to be caused by living spirit beings.

That is the tragedy of psychology attempting to deal with spiritual problems. It mis-understands the causes of what they are seeing, so it does not at all treat the real causes: all they can do is attempt to "counsel" the person into behaving "properly" and/or prescribe "medications" (drugs) to "relieve the symptoms". So, it mis-diagnoses the real problem as its observed behavior or malfunction (depression or anger/hostility) and then also mis-treats it.

Essentially, I submit to you that psychology just plain mis-ses the whole scenario. The reason is that psychology <u>deals with spiritual enemies with physical, chemical and intellectual counseling</u>. In other words, the Bible would call this *__fighting a spiritual warfare with carnal weapons__* (Ephesians 6:12, 2 Corinthians 10:4, 5).

Not only is doing this anti-Scriptural, it is also, therefore, highly ineffective.

"Psychology" is Not From God

I hope you realize the impact of the above statements and Scriptures. They reveal that the weapons of our warfare have to be "not carnal" and only then are they "mighty through God" to pull down and cast down everything that exalts itself against the knowledge of God. Do you see that this would include almost everything that psychology holds as fundamental?

The essence of the issue is that most "psychology" is not derived from Scripture. Most psychology is <u>totally separate from Scriptural truths, principles,</u>

doctrines and teachings. Therefore, it has no "Scriptural solutions". As seen above, it only offers solutions devised based on a non-Scriptural understanding of how man functions.

I submit to you that if God is our Creator and Maker, then He knows best how we are made and how we are designed to function. He also tells us what is afflicting us. He did not leave us ignorant or lacking the Truth that we need to know: about how we are made, our make-up, our needs, how our Maker provides for proper functioning based on His design **and also about the real situation regarding our real enemies**. I submit to you that it is as Jesus said: "Thy Word is Truth" (John 17:17).

Therefore, it is folly and foolishness to try to "fix" a spiritual being (man) afflicted with spiritual attacks by evils spirits with non-spiritual means that only address the **non-spiritual results on the soul and the body**. It is **sheer nonsense**. Do you think it is God's will for such "solutions" from psychology? Absolutely not.

Solutions from "psychology" result from lack of knowledge of the Truth (Hosea 4:6, 7). Further, we who call ourselves "believers" must realize that "psychology", at its root and core, is not a result of God's provided "health and wholeness plan". **It is the devil's substitute plan.**

The basic, secular understanding of man's root issues and "**the sources**" of "thoughts and emotions" in most of what is commonly known as "psychology" is **an alternate understanding of man** which is **totally separate from God's Truth and "Owner's Manual"...which is God's Word, the Bible.**

In fact, one of psychology's "founding fathers" looked to find answers to man's problems after he failed to find answers through religion. In his early writings, he plainly states that he had **a spirit guide** that showed him about other spirits working over us, which he later marginalized and simply called the "archetypes and dark shadows of our ancestral darkness". Another founding father of psychology **also went in a direction opposite to God** and sought answers from humanism, intellectualism and philosophy, all the while using drugs for "enhancing" human intellectual performance and potential. **When they went in that direction, away from God's answers, they found a whole other set of answers**. I suggest to you that instead of God's answers and Truth, they found **a whole world of lies**. And I further allege to you that those lies were **given to them by the father of lies** (John 8:44), **who was all too ready and eager to provide these men, and the world** *through them and their teachings*, **an alternate version of the Truth of God.**

Remember Genesis 3:1: "...*yeah, hath God said...?*"

Yes, the enemy, the father of lies, was more than glad to give these "fathers of psychology" **a whole other set of answers**. "Yea, hath God said you 'wrestle not flesh and blood but...'? No. You wrestle the subconscious, the Id, the Ego, the Superego, repressed desires, oral fixation issues, manic-depression, schizophrenia, Oedipus complex, maternal issues, paternal issues, stool training and retentive issues, etc". The father of lies went on and on with more "alternate truths": he told these men about "personality profiles" and "behavior modification" and "biofeedback" and "emotional states" and on and on and on.

The Scripture that comes to mind is:

> **Colossians 2:18b ...intruding into those things which he hath not seen, <u>vainly puffed up by his fleshly mind</u>,**

These men came up with these elaborate ideas and systems of thought all apart from God; it was all "vainly puffed up" by their carnal minds which were not led by God's Spirit but by other spirits, bringing all kinds of "erroneous conclusions and doctrines" that include angel worship and every other error, no matter how "right" it may seem.

> **Proverbs 14:12 There is a way which seemeth right unto a man, but the end thereof [are] the ways of death.**

And the very same Words again:

> **Proverbs 16:25 There is a way that seemeth right unto a man, but the end thereof [are] the ways of death.**

Even if we think we are right, no matter how right it **seems, if it is not from God, it does not lead to life or success.**

And Hosea 4:6 also seems particularly fitting:

> **Hosea 4:6 My people are destroyed for lack of knowledge: <u>because thou hast rejected knowledge</u>, I will also reject thee, that thou shalt be no priest to me: seeing thou hast forgotten the law of thy God, I will also forget thy children.**

Whatever knowledge we may have or think we have, **if it is not from God, it is likely incorrect and not true...for it is not His Truth.** And, **when we reject God's knowledge, we are destroyed because we lack His knowledge, which is the only Truth.**

You see, **no good ever comes when we depart from God's Truth.** Not only are we disobedient, which disqualifies us from His blessings and instead qualifies us for His curses (Deuteronomy 28), **we will never obtain the best or the right results if we follow an "owner's manual" from anyone other than our "Original Equipment Manufacturer".**

As stated above, **God alone is our Creator and Maker** and **He alone knows best how we are designed** and therefore, **how we can "function optimally**".

Scriptures About Spiritual Enemies – Revisited with Psychology

In this next section, we will revisit some of the Scriptural passages we saw in Chapter 2, as well as some other ones, and look at them from a psychological point of view to evaluate how effective the psychological view and treatment would be in comparison to the approach and actions that Jesus, Paul and others took.

1. Mark 9:17-29 – Jesus heals the scribe's son

In this passage, a scribe brought his son to the disciples and sought that they would cast out of him a dumb spirit which would take the son and tear at him, cause him to foam at the mouth, gnash with his teeth and become rigid. When the spirit saw Jesus, it tare at the child to where the child fell to the ground and wallowed foaming. The father adds that sometimes the spirit would throw the child into the fire or into waters to destroy him.

Jesus' approach: Jesus asked to father of the child to believe and spoke to him that "all things are possible to him that believes". And after, the father replies with tears: "Lord, I believe".

> **Mark 9:25 When Jesus saw that the people came running together, he rebuked the foul spirit, saying unto him, [Thou] dumb and deaf spirit, I charge thee, come out of him, and enter no more into him.**
> **26 And [the spirit] cried, and rent him sore, and came out of him: and he was as one dead; insomuch that many said, He is dead.**
> **27 But Jesus took him by the hand, and lifted him up; and he arose.**

Jesus **rebuked** the foul spirit, **recognizing** it was a dumb and deaf spirit, and **commanded** it to come out of him **and return no more** unto the child. Though the spirit rent the child and was as dead to many, the spirit left and Jesus took the child by the hand, lifted him and the child arose.

The **result** was a total healing and deliverance form the spiritual root of all the physical and emotional problems.

Psychological approach: After observing a child that foams at the mouth, gnashes with his teeth, becomes rigid, falls to the ground and wallows foaming and sometimes "throws himself" into fire or waters to attempt "self-destruction", the diagnosis would probably be epilepsy, involuntary muscular spasms and tightening, loss of muscular control or coordination and/or even suicidal tendencies. Treatment might include restraints, drug therapy, and/or counseling for suicidal tendencies.

The **results** of this approach are likely **multiple visits** to psychologists or psychiatrists for **observations, evaluations and counseling** plus the **expenses for these visits and for the drug treatments.**

2. Luke 4:33-37 – Man with unclean spirit manifests at synagogue in Capernaum

In this passage, Jesus is teaching on the Shabbat day and the people were astonished at His doctrine and His word was with power. The man with the unclean devil cried out with a loud voice.

Jesus' approach: Jesus simply rebukes the spirit and commands him out of the man. Though the spirit throws down the man, the spirit comes out and does not hurt the man.

The **result** is that the man is completely delivered and set free from the spiritual oppressor.

Psychological approach: If this happened in a congregation today, the man would likely be promptly escorted out of the congregation to avoid disrupting the order of the service and referred to a psychologist or other "specialist" who might counsel the man for his disruptive and improper behavior and perhaps prescribe sedatives or other drugs to help control his behavior.

Again, the **result** is likely multiple visits for counseling and the expense for the consultations and the drugs being prescribed.

3. Luke 13: 10-17 – The woman that had a spirit of infirmity 18 years and was bowed

I must write here that, even as I read this portion of Scripture and prepared to summarize and write about this passage without including all of it, as above, and continue with other passages below, I was impacted strongly by the Spirit of the Living God and strongly impressed to, instead, just include the whole passage straight from the Holy Word of God **and let the Living Word, the same Living Messiah of Whom these Words are written, speak for Himself, again, even as He Himself did on that day at that synagogue!**

> **Luke 13:10 And he was teaching in one of the synagogues on the Sabbath.**
> **11 And, behold, there was a woman which had a spirit of infirmity eighteen years, and was bowed together, and could in no wise lift up [herself].**
> **12 And when Jesus saw her, he called [her to him], and said unto her, Woman, thou art loosed from thine infirmity.**
> **13 And he laid [his] hands on her: and immediately she was made straight, and glorified God.**
> **14 And the ruler of the synagogue answered with indignation, because that Jesus had healed on the Sabbath day, and said unto the people, There are six days in which men ought to work: in them**

therefore come and be healed, and not on the Sabbath day.
15 The Lord then answered him, and said, [Thou] hypocrite, doth not each one of you on the Sabbath loose his ox or [his] ass from the stall, and lead [him] away to watering?
16 And ought not this woman, being a daughter of Abraham, whom Satan hath bound, lo, these eighteen years, be loosed from this bond on the Sabbath day?
17 And when he had said these things, all his adversaries were ashamed: and all the people rejoiced for all the glorious things that were done by him.

I am also strongly impressed that I am to point out certain powerful highlights of this account as 'His footnote", **so that the Spirit of the Living God may pierce our hearts with the powerful truths of this passage, which epitomize the concepts being set forth in this chapter**!

In this passage, we see the Son of the Living God, full of the power and discernment and wisdom of the Spirit of God, encounter a daughter of Abraham, His covenant people, whom He loves, who has been afflicted with **a spirit of infirmity**, *a spirit that is not of God*, that has resulted in the woman being bowed and not able to lift herself.

When Jesus saw her, He called her to Him and He laid hands on her and spoke to her: *"you are loosed from your infirmity"*. **Immediately**, she was made straight. And she glorified God!

Jesus had no need for a medical doctor, orthopedic surgeon nor a chiropractor that day. He simply **dealt with the spirit of infirmity** and **spoke** and **declared** that she was loosed from her infirmity (spirit) as He laid hands on her! Immediately, she was made straight, which was of such significance for her that the woman **immediately praised God**, for what was done unto her! And rightly so!

Oh, readers: are you not touched with the love and compassion with which Jesus was touched as He loosed this woman from that spirit that had her so afflicted for so long?

But that was not all that we see in this passage. We then see that, not only did God work a mighty miracle, but that even a "godly man", the leader of the synagogue, rather than be glad for the woman and also glorify God, was moved with **indignation** and had the **thoughts** that this should have happened not on the Shabbat but rather on one of the other six days!

From what we have learned so far in this book, we see that **this man was yielded to thoughts of legalism** and **feelings of indignation** towards those that do not follow *what he deemed to be "the right procedure"*. Obviously, **a spirit that was not of love and wisdom or from God** was in control of this man at that moment and **acted out** <u>its nature</u> **through that man**.

To which the Lord replied with the powerful words in verses 15 and 16! He discerned the **hypocrisy** (thoughts and feelings and actions and "attitude"- another spirit!) in the man and pointed it out to the man and for all those present to understand.

The Lord also clarifies that this woman, being a daughter of Abraham, ought to be loosed on the

Shabbat, more so than an ox or ass, after being **bound by Satan** eighteen years!

The results are in verse 17: **His adversaries were ashamed** and **all the people** (the others, **the "non-adversaries" of the Lord**) rejoiced! Why? **"For all the glorious things that were done by Him"**!

*Oh, readers, don't you see, sense and hear **what the Spirit is saying?***

> **What this chapter has been trying to convey is that the Lord does not just want us to follow a manner of procedure that comes <u>from what the carnal mind thinks</u> is God's way or procedure or method or <u>that has limits which are deemed right by a mind that is apart from the Living God and His wisdom and His Spirit!</u>**
>
> **He was manifested to destroy the works of the devil, no matter what those works may be!**
>
> **And He does not "play with the enemy" <u>nor does He avoid confronting him!</u> He is God Almighty and has decreed and manifested the Son of Man and the Son of God on earth to do exactly that: to destroy the works of the devil on this earth; works that have been worked <u>since he gained access into this world!</u> (Romans 5:12.)**
>
> **And He is <u>absolutely telling us</u>, <u>and calling us</u>, to walk <u>in the power</u> and <u>the authority</u> of the redemption of the Almighty, which he**

Himself purchased for us through His blood! (Colossians 1:14.)

Jesus said we would do even greater and mightier works than these! (John 14:12.) He also is telling us that devils ARE SUBJECT UNTO US IN HIS NAME and that He has given US His power and authority over serpents and scorpions and over all the power of the enemy and nothing shall by any means hurt us! (Luke 10:17-19.)

He is telling us that He IS calling us, His people, HIS BODY ON THIS EARTH...to GO FORTH, BOLDLY, and DO the works of God, the greater works, which WE ARE COMMANDED to DO!

For HE DESIRES that these works BE DONE! That the sick be healed, that the DEAD BE RAISED, that DEVILS BE CAST OUT! That the LEPERS BE CLEANSED!

He is telling us that He has indeed called us, HIS ARMY, to BE...HIS ARMY...ON THE EARTH...and SHOW FORTH HIS PRAISE...AND HIS POWER...and to DEMONSTRATE IT...so that, as in the above passage:

That ALL THE PEOPLE MAY GLORIFY GOD AND REJOICE FOR ALL THE GLORIOUS THINGS THAT SHALL BE DONE BY HIM!

4

RECOGNIZING GOD'S MASTER PLAN

In the last chapter, we looked at how **ineffective** it would be and is to attempt **to deal with spiritual issues and a spiritual enemy as if they were "psychological issues".** We stated that such would essentially be **using non-spiritual, carnal weapons for our warfare**. That is because psychology is a whole other framework of understanding that is separate from, and does not come from, the Word of God.

And, since that is so, is it any wonder that such a framework would be so ineffective?

We plainly stated that any "knowledge", other than God's knowledge, is simply inferior. At best, it might only yield inferior results. At worst, it will cause utter failure and death. That is because it often causes us to "miss the mark" **and miss the real target.**

In the case and focus of this book, **it causes us to miss the real enemy altogether**. Our target has to be the enemy that has us targeted. **Missing and not hitting the enemy in a war is catastrophic and inevitably leads to being killed in battle**.

If we can't hit the enemy, we cannot defeat him. And if we cannot defeat him, he will eventually defeat us.

Therefore, I submit to you that **we cannot afford to have any other "battle plan" other than that which is from God.** And as we saw, **psychology is not God's battle plan**.

So what is God's battle plan? Do we have such a plan? Where do we go to get it? Did God leave us without a battle plan? An *effective* battle plan? *His* battle plan?

We Do Have God's Plan...But Are We Really Using It?

We need to realize some "basic Bible truths" and then realize that though we may "know these things", that it is **an absolute must for us to use God's ways, and only God's ways, if we are to have the best chances of success in our warfare**.

We need to remember and focus on **the absolute need** of 2 Corinthians 10:4 again:

> **2 Corinthians 10:4 (For the weapons of our warfare [are] not carnal, but mighty through God to the pulling down of strong holds;)**

The weapons of our warfare *cannot be carnal...in any way, shape or form.*

This could be said to be one of the causes of the problem that I referred to in the introduction.

We have already begun to see what that problem is and what the solution is. We will soon get to the specifics of implementing the solution. I now continue **to clarify the root causes for that big problem.** And by identifying the root causes, we will remedy the problem as we implement the cure and remove those things that are causing the problem.

One reason that we are not recognizing the enemy *enough* and we are not removing the enemy *enough* is that we are not using God's Understanding and Plan *enough.*

We have been deceived by the deceiver **into mixing with the Word of God just about every other plan there is to man**. Psychology is just one of the things that we have been deceived into "mixing in" with our battle plan from God. **The result** is that those ingredients, being sneaked in to us by the deceiver, have **not only diluted the potency of our warfare and our battle plan, they have also poisoned it...and have even deluded us into targeting just about everything else besides the real enemy**.

Imagine a war in which we do not track, target and eliminate the enemy. Imagine that, instead, we only sought to tend to the wounded, rebuild blown up buildings and equipment or build new ones; build and transport supplies for the war; train soldiers for the war. And did everything else associated with a war...**except that we did not search for, find nor kill the enemy.** *What kind of war would that be? What kind of victory would we have?* It would be insane and ridiculous. And, of course, **we would not achieve victory**. We would essentially be at the mercy of the enemy's ability to wipe us out. Our longevity would only be determined by the enemy's ability to kill us.

That is exactly the war we are often fighting today. **We are not even seeing the real enemy**. So, we are not tracking him nor identifying his location. **Nor are we shooting directly at him with weaponry that is adequate or capable of destroying him**. It goes without saying that we cannot win a war like that. **We will be "dead meat" if we do not correct the way the war is being fought.**

What makes the above scenario worse, if such a thing is possible, is that **the same lack** of understanding and sound, accurate intelligence information that we are basing our warfare on **is also guiding (or rather, mis-guiding) the way we treat our wounded** and **train our soldiers** for battle!

Please consider very carefully the following statements: Just like in times past, not knowing about bacteria, infections and surgical methods led to massive amputations and ineffective treatment in the field and in the hospitals of battle, we in the hospitals of spiritual battles (the churches and congregations) are often amputating limbs, mistreating all kinds of spiritual wounds **and losing soldiers and lives** because **we do not even see and recognize the "spiritual bacteria"**. Let me put it to you this way: *As living but invisible bacteria once were for physical wounds, so are evil spirits now for spiritual wounds.*

And, we are training the "replacement soldiers" to use the same battle plan that previous soldiers have been using, which is **doomed to fail** also, **because it does not recognize, identify, target, shoot nor kill the enemy!** All we are doing is training our soldiers to go out and tend to the wounded but ignore the spiritual bacteria. And to build churches and recruit soldiers (evangelize) and study war manuals (the Bible, **but mixed with** many other "theological studies" that often are full of the very ingredients from the enemy, through often well-meaning but deceived men, that dilute and even poison our only effective battle plan) **instead of learning how to recognize the real enemy** and **then find and kill (meaning, remove or cast out) the enemy.**

We Must Take a Closer Look at God's Plan and Revise Our Warfare

I trust that by now you see the point I am making. It is simply this: **because the enemy has been so successful at hiding the fact that we are fighting him and his evil spirits** that are **alive** and **that _affect_ and _infect_ our lives and our wounds** (which is the essence of his attack upon us), **we are largely not even seeing, targeting nor removing and defeating him enough.**

The enemy has succeeded at taking our eyes off the "keys to the warfare" in the Word of God and has substituted a whole other "culprit" to our problems, our lives and our battles **and then also substituted a whole other set of "solutions"** to those culprits. **We think our problems and our culprits are everything and everyone else...except the enemy and his evil kingdom of evil spirits.** And we try to remedy all of that with psychology, doctors and every other "good idea" and everything else...**except God's ways that come expressly from God's Truth and God's Manual.**

This madness, wrought by the deceptive enemy, **must stop if** we are to be the victorious army that we are supposed to be. And, we will be that, not because we are just saying it, but because HE is able, and HE really IS making us be what we need to be.

This has started to come to pass because it is **HE that is truly revealing to us the madness as well as the remedy: returning to His Battle Plan, the only true, effective and winning plan.**

We Must Follow His Master Plan If We Want to Win

As stated earlier, one big reason we have been deceived into not seeing the enemy for who he and his army really are is that we have not been guided expressly by the sound and accurate information that can only be found in God's Word. His Word is Truth (John 17:17). **Therefore, any other "explanations" about what afflicts us, what our problems are or what the solutions might be are absolute lies.** When psychology or any other "school of thought" attempts to tell us something, we should check it against the Word of God and really see if it is **pure**, or if it is **truth mixed with a little lie**, which is still a big lie. We must be like the Bereans and we must **only** allow **God** to be **True.**

> **Romans 3:4 God forbid: yea, let God be true, but every man a liar; as it is written, That thou mightest be justified in thy sayings, and mightest overcome when thou art judged.**

> **Acts 17:10 And the brethren immediately sent away Paul and Silas by night unto Berea: who**

coming [thither] went into the synagogue of the Jews.
11 These were more noble than those in Thessalonica, in that they received the word with all readiness of mind, and searched the scriptures daily, whether those things were so.

We must receive the Word of God with all readiness, instead of every other "new thing" that comes along that has no solid Scriptural base. Not all "new teachings" are bad or false, but we must be discerning to the Spirit and also search the Scriptures to ensure that anything "new to us" is actually in the Scriptures and does not contradict sound Scriptural doctrine, just as when Paul taught the Bereans. We must never place anything **above** the Word of God **nor accept what the Word rejects.**

If we had searched the Scriptures more, perhaps we might have seen **that the whole psychological approach to man's problems does not fit with Scriptures and is "a whole other framework".** Perhaps we would be clearer about **the methods that Jesus demonstrated when He met and discerned the enemy and evil spirits *among us*.**

Unfortunately, the enemy is **a deceiver and is a very subtle one** (Genesis 3:1), so he has been able to **hide from us even his and his army's living, thinking nature and presence within us** and deceive us into **thinking that we alone are "the problem", instead of him and his army in and through us.**

It is time to get him and his army out of us! That is the only truly effective way to stop them from working upon and through us. Praise be to God for spitting in our eyes and laying hands on us again so we may see more clearly! (Mark 8:22-25.)

God's Word IS God's Master Plan – for Everything

Therefore, let us realize, again, and once and for all, that God's Word is Truth. It is the purest form of knowledge there is for man. It is mankind's "owner's manual" for the product called man. *(Once again, as stated in the "Acknowledgements", I give credit to Dr. Myles Munroe for this analogy of how God is our "Manufacturer" and how His Word is our "Owner's Manual" to help us operate optimally. Elements of his teachings are used in these two sections through the end of the chapter.)*

In the same way that an earthly manufacturer includes an owner's manual with every TV, VCR or tape recorder it makes, God Almighty is **our heavenly Manufacturer**. And, in His wisdom and love for us, He did not neglect to give us also **our "Owner's Manual"**. Why? For the same reasons that earthly manufacturers include such a manual: **so that we can <u>properly operate, use, enjoy and receive optimal performance and all the capabilities from a given device</u>**. In order to do that, there are things we must know about it in order to **operate it properly** and have it **function the way it is supposed to**.

It is the same with us. **Only the Maker** knows exactly how we are made. **Only He knows exactly** how we operate optimally and **what we require**. And, **when we malfunction, He alone is "Factory Authorized"** to refurbish us and restore us to "good as new" condition and then return us to service. Hallelujah!

As our Maker, God knows the truth about our components and knows what, **and who**, is a real enemy to us, our components and our lives.

- **Only His Manual has the Truth** about **how we began, how we were made and who attacked us from the beginning and has been attacking us ever since**.
- **Only His Manual** tells us **who**, _not what_, came to steal, kill and destroy and who opposes God and His people (remember that Satan means "adversary").
- **Only His Manual** tells us **the details** of the attacks against us, our lives, our relationships, our walk with God, our holiness, our health and our mission on this earth.
- **Only His Manual** tells us how to win the battle that we are called to. And only His Manual tells us how to defeat the enemy and **how to fix anything and everything that goes wrong** along the way.

That is why we must make His Manual the highest Manual in our lives with Him.

**God's Manual, God's Word, is God's Master Plan.**

His Word is:

- His winning battle plan for our warfare;
- His winning plan for our individual lives to be full of His abundant life;

- His winning plan for us to enjoy a walk of holiness and communion with Him; and
- His winning plan for relationships, for health, and for being everything He has called us to be.

It is His winning plan for everything related to our lives' design. He designed us and made us precisely as designed. And He also designed what our lives should be like.

Joshua 1:8 This book of the law shall not depart out of thy mouth; but thou shalt meditate therein day and night, that thou mayest observe to do according to all that is written therein: for then thou shalt make thy way prosperous, and then thou shalt have good success.
9 Have not I commanded thee? Be strong and of a good courage; be not afraid, neither be thou dismayed: for the LORD thy God [is] with thee whithersoever thou goest.

John 10:10 The thief cometh not, but for to steal, and to kill, and to destroy: I am come that they might have life, and that they might have [it] more abundantly.

John 15:4 Abide in me, and I in you. As the branch cannot bear fruit of itself, except it abide in the vine; no more can ye, except ye abide in me.
5 I am the vine, ye [are] the branches: He that abideth in me, and I in him, the same bringeth forth much fruit: for without me ye can do nothing.
6 If a man abide not in me, he is cast forth as a branch, and is withered; and men gather them, and cast [them] into the fire, and they are burned.

7 If ye abide in me, and my words abide in you, ye shall ask what ye will, and it shall be done unto you.

By design and by operating specifications, as the Scriptures above show, **we can do nothing without Him**. We must abide in Him *or else we malfunction*. His Words and His Law show us the way to be successful, have good success and are the way to abide in Him and for Him to abide in us. If we do not abide in Him, we cannot have His abundant life.

When Our Enemies Are In Our Lives, We Show a Malfunction

If any area of our lives does not conform to His Manual, we are, as a device, "malfunctioning".

If a device must have electricity at 110 volts but you try to run it on 220 volts, it will be "fried". If it needs to be in a cool, dry environment but you use it in a hot, humid environment, it will not operate optimally and may eventually break down. If it must be kept away from liquids and direct sunlight but you violate these conditions, you will not obtain optimal results at best and you may get no results at all at worst. The device may eventually even become "inoperable".

It is the same way with us, God's "living device". We are designed to **operate optimally _only when_** we follow God's Manual (obey His Word) <u>and are connected</u> to His prescribed power source (Him) <u>and operate in the environment</u> He prescribed for us (His presence, love, joy, peace, etc.) <u>and in the manner</u> that He designed and intended.

If we lack any of those prescribed specifications and/**or bring in things that are not prescribed or known to have adverse effects**, our operation suffers and **we malfunction.**

<u>**In the next few chapters, we will focus on how the Body of Messiah is malfunctioning**</u>, as stated in the introduction to this book, <u>so we can understand</u> the malfunctions, <u>identify</u> the conditions and intruders causing the malfunctions, and quickly go on to correct the conditions, <u>remove</u> the intruders <u>**and restore ourselves to the optimal functioning that our loving Maker, Designer and Manufacturer always intended.**</u>

5

WHO IS LIVING
IN OUR TEMPLE?

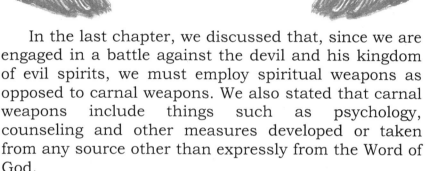

In the last chapter, we discussed that, since we are engaged in a battle against the devil and his kingdom of evil spirits, we must employ spiritual weapons as opposed to carnal weapons. We also stated that carnal weapons include things such as psychology, counseling and other measures developed or taken from any source other than expressly from the Word of God.

We also realized that it has been the enemy who seeks to deceive us into **strategies and plans** that "seem good" or "sound good" but are **not from God and His Word** in order to lead us into using **methods that are less effective, or altogether ineffective**, in **dealing with him and the damage, infiltration and spiritual wounds perpetrated by his evil spirits in our lives**. He also <u>seeks to direct our focus</u> **away from himself as the true enemy** and **to avoid being targeted.**

We also realized that the deception into employing misguided battle plans and remedies to the damages received in our battles with the enemy is another result of not focusing expressly on using God's weapons and strategies which come from the truths and principles given to us by God in His Word, which we identified as His "Master Plan" for everything in our lives, for it identifies **our real enemy and God's way to defeat him**, as well as God's prescription, remedy and answer to everything in our lives.

> **2 Peter 1:3 According as his divine power hath given unto us all things that [pertain] unto life and godliness, through the knowledge of him that hath called us to glory and virtue:**

In this chapter, we will focus on a **key ingredient that God has given to us in His Master Plan in order to lead us to victory in every area of our lives**: **the Holy Spirit**, given to us to **dwell in us**. While this fact may not be new to believers, it is critical and indispensable that we **clarify some key aspects about Him**, which we may have never realized before, if we are to have the victory in any area of our lives.

We will look closely at the key things that the Holy Spirit provides for us and how they are **crucial** for us to achieve the total victory that is currently eluding the Body of Messiah.

And the "second part" of this chapter will be of amazing impact: we will see just how **crucial** it is for us to more clearly **recognize the Holy Spirit:** *in order to more clearly recognize the enemy*...**the moment they begin to "inject"** *their* **"thoughts and feelings and emotions" into us**! We must recognize this the moment it starts to happen, so we can come against them, and not get carried along by them (their "thoughts and emotions") into accepting and acting these out, which <u>then becomes "our"</u> sin. *Please read on with open hearts and minds, for this is crucial!*

We Cannot Defeat Evil Spirits Without the Holy Spirit

Since we have learned and isolated the very important Truth and fact that our enemy is not flesh and blood but rather evil **spirits** that operate through flesh-and-blood (Ephesians 6:12), it should be obvious to us that **we in our flesh** cannot do anything, much less defeat, these **evil spirits** which are our **spiritual** enemies. So, we must keep extracting from Scripture, God's winning Master Plan, the rest of His keys to victory and success on **how to defeat spirits**. Our Master, Teacher and Savior <u>showed us how</u>.

> **Luke 11:20 But if I with the finger of God cast out devils, no doubt the kingdom of God is come upon you.**

Jesus said this in response to questions and accusations about His casting out evil spirits. He told us *how* He was casting out the devils. So, if Jesus Himself, as man on earth, demonstrated to us how He did it, we **also must do it the way He did it** and follow His example instead of attempting to come up with "a better way", for **there is never a better way for anything than <u>His way</u>.**

He did it only <u>by</u> and <u>through</u> the Holy Spirit that was given to Him, that had descended upon Him and that He was anointed with.

> **Luke 3:22 And the Holy Ghost descended in a bodily shape like a dove upon him, and a voice came from heaven, which said, Thou art my beloved Son; in thee I am well pleased.**

> **Luke 4:18** The Spirit of the Lord [is] upon me, because he hath anointed me to preach the gospel to the poor; he hath sent me to heal the brokenhearted, to preach deliverance to the captives, and recovering of sight to the blind, to set at liberty them that are bruised,
> **19** To preach the acceptable year of the Lord.

> **Zechariah 4:6** Then he answered and spake unto me, saying, This [is] the word of the LORD unto Zerubbabel, saying, Not by might, nor by power, but by my spirit, saith the LORD of hosts.

> **Acts 1:8** But ye shall receive power, after that the Holy Ghost is come upon you: and ye shall be witnesses unto me both in Jerusalem, and in all Judaea, and in Samaria, and unto the uttermost part of the earth.

Do you see? Jesus received the Holy Ghost upon Himself upon being baptized and soon after, He explained the purpose for His being anointed with the Spirit of the Lord. Not only did that passage fulfill Isaiah 61:1-2, it also corroborates that **it is not by anything else but by His Spirit.** And, Jesus told His disciples to wait for the promise of Holy Spirit so that they would receive **the same power**.

This is the **power** they would need **in order to succeed** in the Great Commission and **to be victorious** in the things they would encounter. It was **spiritual** power, from the mighty Holy **Spirit** of God, that they would need if they were to defeat the evil **spirits** that they would encounter and have to battle. **It is the same with us ever since and even now**: <u>we have to *"fight spirit with Spirit"*.</u>

Why Else Do We Need the Holy Spirit?

Now that we have seen perhaps the most basic reason why **we have to battle spirits with a Spirit instead of the flesh**, let us look at a few more crucial reasons why God gave us the Holy Spirit to indwell us.

1. He guides us unto all Truth.

As we have already seen, we **need to have God's Word/Truth** (John 17:17) about everything if we are **to avoid being deceived** by the enemy about all kinds of things. The enemy deceived Adam and Eve by questioning God's Word. If we don't know or remember God's Truth, we are then vulnerable to **not discerning or recognizing a lie when we hear it *in thoughts, feelings, emotions* or in spoken words**.

> **John 16:13 Howbeit when he, the Spirit of truth, is come, he will guide you into all truth: for he shall not speak of himself; but whatsoever he shall hear, [that] shall he speak: and he will shew you things to come.**

2. He is our Comforter and the Spirit of Truth.

Jesus called Him "another Comforter", meaning, another One **like Himself** to walk with us and be with us. In fact, He even pointed out that the Holy Spirit would **dwell with us** and be **in us**.

> **John 14:16 And I will pray the Father, and he shall give you another Comforter, that he may abide with you <u>for ever</u>;**
> **17 [Even] the Spirit of truth; whom the world cannot receive, because it seeth him not,**

neither knoweth him: but ye know him; for he dwelleth <u>with you</u>, and shall be <u>in you</u>.

3. He is our Comforter and teaches us all things and reminds us of His Words.

Jesus said that the Holy Spirit would teach us **all** things. Only God, by His Spirit, can and does teach us the things we need to know **to do things "God's way"**.

The Spirit also **reminds us of Jesus' words** and teachings. The Holy Spirit speaks God's Word.

> **John 14:26 But the Comforter, [which is] the Holy Ghost, whom the Father will send in my name, he shall teach you all things, and bring all things to your remembrance, whatsoever I have said unto you.**

4. He will teach us what to say when we need to know what God wants us to say.

Jesus told us that the Holy Spirit would instantly tell us and teach us what to say in situations such as what to answer when taken before rulers or authorities. How very reassuring!

> **Luke 12:11 And when they bring you unto the synagogues, and [unto] magistrates, and powers, take ye no thought how or what thing ye shall answer, or what ye shall say:**
> **12 For the Holy Ghost shall teach you in the same hour what ye ought to say.**

> **Acts 4:5 And it came to pass on the morrow, that their rulers, and elders, and scribes,**
> **6 And Annas the high priest, and Caiaphas, and John, and Alexander, and as many as were of the**

kindred of the high priest, were gathered together at Jerusalem.

7 And when they had set them in the midst, they asked, By what power, or by what name, have ye done this?

8 Then Peter, filled with the Holy Ghost, said unto them, Ye rulers of the people, and elders of Israel,

9 If we this day be examined of the good deed done to the impotent man, by what means he is made whole;

10 Be it known unto you all, and to all the people of Israel, that by the name of Jesus Christ of Nazareth, whom ye crucified, whom God raised from the dead, [even] by him doth this man stand here before you whole.

5. He leads and guides the Body of Believers as they carry out Jesus' Commission and seek God's counsel in making decisions.

God has given us examples of how we are to proceed when we need to make important decisions in the Body or when questions arise about proper doctrine.

> Acts 15:28 For it seemed good to the Holy Ghost, and to us, to lay upon you no greater burden than these necessary things;

6. He speaks to men through the mouths of the prophets.

Let me say something briefly on this point: I am shocked at the **excessive** amount of skepticism in the Body against prophets. I absolutely agree that there is great falsehood in this area...*but so is there in other functions in the Body like teachers and pastors as well.*

But if there's **one** function that is **highly accused** and folks are **most skeptical of**, it has to be the office and function of the prophet. **And this ought not to be so.**

There is also a great deal of false currency in the world. And despite that, we do not think money counterfeit as the "first reaction". Yet that seems to be the only reaction and opinion about prophets sometimes. **I say: let us test the spirits and prove all things, hold on to that which is good and quench not the Spirit and despise not prophesyings.**

> **1 Thessalonians 5:19 Quench not the Spirit.**
> **20 Despise not prophesyings.**
> **21 Prove all things; hold fast that which is good.**

I know that a lot of folks have been hurt and misled by false prophets or false prophecies. But realize that we have all been hurt by all kinds of folks...and we can't write everyone off just because of that. **We need to be** more **mature and discerning** than that.

Let us not be so "turned off" that we become "anti-prophets" or "anti-prophecies", **because it would be the enemy that would love that the most if we did!**

Realize that prophets are of God and are of great value to the Body when these men and women hear from the Lord. Scriptures bear this out:

> **Acts 13:1 Now there were in the church that was at Antioch certain prophets and teachers; as Barnabas, and Simeon that was called Niger, and Lucius of Cyrene, and Manaen, which had been brought up with Herod the tetrarch, and Saul.**

> 2 As they ministered to the Lord, and fasted, the Holy Ghost said, Separate me Barnabas and Saul for the work whereunto I have called them.
> 3 And when they had fasted and prayed, and laid [their] hands on them, they sent [them] away.
> 4 So they, being sent forth by the Holy Ghost, departed unto Seleucia; and from thence they sailed to Cyprus.

In the verses above, we see that "they" (these men) minister to the Lord, fast, pray, and speak what "the Holy Ghost said", and they lay their hands on them and sent men away...**and yet Scripture says those sent away were sent by the Holy Ghost!**

Again I say: **let us be mature and discerning,** so that when "the real dollar bill" comes along, **we see, recognize and not "throw away" a real dollar bill for fear and skepticism.**

Another example is seen in the life of Paul. Some might question "why the great apostle Paul would need some prophet to tell him anything!" (I have personally heard such skepticism and more.) Well, Scripture shows us it happened at least on this one instance:

> Acts 21:10 And as we tarried [there] many days, there came down from Judaea a certain prophet, named Agabus.
> 11 And when he was come unto us, he took Paul's girdle, and bound his own hands and feet, and said, Thus saith the Holy Ghost, So shall the Jews at Jerusalem bind the man that owneth this girdle, and shall deliver [him] into the hands of the Gentiles.

The point is that Scripture bears out that prophets played their role in the early, Spirit-filled believers...and nothing suggests that such would not continue to be **needful and beneficial.**

> **Acts 15:32 And Judas and Silas, being prophets also themselves, exhorted the brethren with many words, and confirmed [them].**

Let us realize that prophets **do exist today and can be of great edification, exhortation and comfort to the Body** of Messiah.

> **1 Corinthians 14:3 But he that prophesieth speaketh unto men [to] edification, and exhortation, and comfort.**

If such are used of the Holy Ghost, do we not want to be led by Him and benefit from His guidance? Do we want to oppose Him, if He so chooses to move in our midst?

7. He reveals to us the things of God.

We stated earlier that God is a Spirit (John 4:24); therefore, only His Spirit can reveal to us things from God. Being spiritual things, they must be spiritually discerned and we in our carnal minds cannot understand, discern nor receive these things.

It is why carnal men with carnal minds, as *intelligent as they may be*, will not receive the Truth from God and will always be in error and is why they have often had "good ideas" but they were not "God ideas", as we saw earlier with psychology and its approach to man's mind, thoughts, emotions, etc.

We must have God's thoughts and insights on the matters we face if we are to **be victorious** and be guided of Him **into the correct decisions. There is no escaping this important fact and it cannot be emphasized enough.**

> **1 Corinthians 2:10 But God hath revealed [them] unto us by his Spirit: for the Spirit searcheth all things, yea, the deep things of God.**
> **11 For what man knoweth the things of a man, save the spirit of man which is in him? even so the things of God knoweth no man, but the Spirit of God.**
> **12 Now we have received, not the spirit of the world, but the spirit which is of God; that we might know the things that are freely given to us of God.**
> **13 Which things also we speak, not in the words which man's wisdom teacheth, but which the Holy Ghost teacheth; comparing spiritual things with spiritual.**
> **14 But the natural man receiveth not the things of the Spirit of God: for they are foolishness unto him: neither can he know [them], because they are spiritually discerned.**

8. **We cannot be God's sons if we are not led of His Spirit.**

It is often said that we are the children of God. And that often implies that we think, feel and act like Him. But, if we are **to have the thoughts, feelings and actions of the Holy Spirit, we have to be led of Him.** According to Scripture, this is a clear "qualification". **Without being led of the Spirit, we can't really claim to be a son of God.**

> **Romans 8:14 For as many as are led by the Spirit of God, they are the sons of God.**

9. He helps us pray according to God's will when we don't know how we should pray so we can receive God's will and God's solutions in our lives.

We stated earlier that we must follow God's Master Plan if we are to be victorious in any area of our lives. **When we are not sure what to do, we can pray for God's will to be done in our lives thanks to the Holy Spirit**, who not only **helps us pray** but also does so **according to God's will. He knows God's will**. We often want God's will in the situations and decisions of our lives even though we are not sure exactly what His will might be. **In those situations, we must have the Holy Spirit.**

> **Romans 8:26 Likewise the Spirit also helpeth our infirmities: for we know not what we should pray for as we ought: but the Spirit itself maketh intercession for us with groanings which cannot be uttered.**
> **27 And he that searcheth the hearts knoweth what [is] the mind of the Spirit, because he maketh intercession for the saints according to [the will of] God.**

10. He helps us present the gospel <u>properly</u> as God desires.

God has specific ideas about how everything should be, including how He is preached and how His gospel is presented. God does not seek to glorify man or man's wisdom, which He considers foolishness. He desires to demonstrate Himself and His power to men to glorify Himself. The Holy Spirit is a crucial and indispensable part of that.

> 1 Corinthians 3:19 For the wisdom of this world is foolishness with God. For it is written, He taketh the wise in their own craftiness.

> 1 Corinthians 2:4 And my speech and my preaching [was] not with enticing words of man's wisdom, but in demonstration of the Spirit and of power:
> 5 That your faith should not stand in the wisdom of men, but in the power of God.

God wants our faith to stand in His power and not in anything of man that is opposite of God's Word and His power. That is a crucial point if we are to have His power working in our lives and through us. It is crucial to understand that so as to remain humble and know that it is **not of us** but it is **all from Him.**

We Have To Do EVERYTHING The Way He Leads and Guides

The above are **just ten of the many reasons** why **we must have the Holy Spirit helping and guiding us**. There are many more. Indeed, as Jesus taught Nicodemus in John Chapter 3, we must be born again of the Spirit or else we can't see the Kingdom of God, understand about the Kingdom of God nor enter into the Kingdom of God.

But the point I'm trying to make here in this chapter and in this book is that **we must have God's guidance** into doing things *exactly* as God would have us do **if we are to be successful** in our lives, in our relationships, in our marriages, in our churches or congregations, in our personal lives, in our jobs, in our ministry or in any and every area of our lives, not to mention the most important part, which is our relationship with our God, Who is to be first and foremost in our lives, Whom we are to love with all our heart, soul, mind and strength and before Whom we are to have no one and no thing (Exodus 20:3, Deuteronomy 6:5, Mark 12:29, 30). Why?

Realize that in all of these areas, we battle the enemy. He attempts to sabotage and ruin every single one of these areas. He came to steal, kill and destroy (John 10:10). He attempts to detour us from the right way in which we should walk, which is in God's Word. He attempts to keep us from walking in God's ways and counsels. Why? Because if we walk in God's ways, we will be blessed and prosperous in everything we do (Joshua 1:8). God gave us His commandments and His ways to walk in "that it might be well with us" (Deuteronomy 5:29).

So, **if the enemy can get us "off track" and away from doing things God's way, we will cease from being blessed and will bring upon ourselves only bad results instead of success.**

And so, by being led of the Spirit of God, discerning the things of God, being shown what to do and say by His Spirit, being taught all things by His Spirit, having His Spirit help us pray according to God's will for our lives and having the power of the Spirit with which to discern the things of the spirit realm and to cast out devils...**will we not increase our chances to be successful in the spiritual battles we face and will face, just as Jesus, Paul and others did? Will we not succeed by the same Spirit of God** the same way they succeeded by the same Spirit of God? **Of course we will. That is God's intention and design all along.**

And **conversely,** *if we do not* approach, discern or handle the spiritual challenges and encounters the same way Jesus, Paul and others did, **but instead** lean into non-Word derived understandings, ideas, theories, procedures and methods that do not proceed from God's Word and do not follow the pattern and the weapons shown to us in God's Word, **we will not succeed**.

We'd end up where we are today: largely **ineffective,** largely **not even seeing the enemy,** largely **not removing the enemy** and largely **suffering the effects of the enemy's damage in our lives, our families and even in our ministries.**

In the next chapters, we will now begin to zero in on just how present the enemy is in our lives and our midst even though the reader at this point may not realize just how present the enemy is. **I assure you that after the next few and to-the-point chapters, the reader will be glad to have read them, for in them the enemy will be exposed like never before**...*so that we may remove him like never before...as God intended all along!* **The time has come in God's timetable for that!**

Now, on the last part of this chapter, let us bring out some of the most powerful insights into the enemy that we can ever get. I promise it will be something that we do not hear taught or preached often, if at all. These are things I did not have anyone tell me as plainly until 2005 and these are things that will shed great light and clarity in helping us recognize and identify the enemy better than ever.

"Part Two": We Are the Temple of God and His Holy Spirit...ONLY?

The above statement may not sound like a new or great revelation right now, **but understanding its fullness will radically change our lives.** It is beyond "great". It is **marvelous.** It is **the main impact of the chapter.**

Sadly, this fact and component of God's design and Master Plan is not understood or appreciated fully even by His Body of believers. We will soon see that it **may be the most crucial piece in helping us recognize our enemy's presence in our lives,** especially when he works **right through ourselves!**

Let us look at two foundational passages of Scripture first.

> **1 Corinthians 3:16 Know ye not that ye are the temple of God, and [that] the Spirit of God dwelleth in you?**
> **17 If any man defile the temple of God, him shall God destroy; for the temple of God is holy, which [temple] ye are.**
>
> **1 Corinthians 6:19 What? know ye not that your body is the temple of the Holy Ghost [which is] in you, which ye have of God, and ye are not your own?**
> **20 For ye are bought with a price: therefore glorify God in your body, and in your spirit, which are God's.**

These Scriptures must become living Truth to us because once they do, they will be more than just another fact about God or just "head knowledge". It has to reach, penetrate and perhaps even pierce our hearts. I trust and pray that the same Spirit that gives us *"revelation about information"* will begin even now to bring to you the same life-changing revelations to you in a very personal way, as He did to me and so many others that were and are being set free by His Spirit and His Truth, that you may also begin to see in a clear way what this book has been promising and anticipating all along. **Prepare your heart and spirit to receive *His* revelations for *your* lives!**

Back to the First Two Chapters

What I and many others had never seen before from the above Scriptures are **the following revelations that are tied together and form a powerful explosion.**

In the first two chapters, we established that thoughts, feelings and actions do not come from dead things but from living beings. We then established that the enemy and his kingdom is the true body of living beings that is actually called "sin" by the Scriptures (Romans 5:12, 7:17-20). Thus, we saw that "sin" is **not just** the act of missing God's mark or the performing of the act that is against God's ways. We saw that sin is **also** alive and *does* the sins. So we see that sin is both the "wrong act" and the living, evil spirits that lead, guide, coach, coax and deceive us into going opposite God's ways and disobeying Him instead of obeying. Are you with me so far? Please stay with me...

Now, we quickly saw how that same body of evil spirits **invaded our world**, starting with Adam and Eve, and invaded all mankind, starting with the two of them, <u>as evidenced by the "negative emotions" (spirits)</u> <u>that they immediately experienced and acted out, like</u> <u>shame, fear, blame and accusation</u>. Their own son Cain <u>soon experienced spirits of envy, jealousy, anger</u> <u>and even murder</u> in slaying his brother Abel. By Genesis Chapter 6, man was so wicked and thought to do evil so continually that God wanted to wipe them all out, and did, in the Flood, except for righteous Noah and his family. **Nevertheless, all that wickedness and disobedience remained unexposed as "unclean spirits", undisturbed and "untormented" on earth unto the coming of Yeshua HaMashiach.**

Now realize that **those evil spirits did not go anywhere. They did not die in the flood. All <u>flesh and blood</u> died. But "evil" remained: <u>"it" (they) just found new people to work through.</u>** <u>They stayed in</u> <u>this world since they entered in the garden and kept</u> <u>harassing mankind ever since.</u> The evidence is that Jesus went about doing good and healing all that were oppressed of the devil (Acts 10:38). He cast out many unclean spirit and devils. He also commanded His disciples (and us) to do the same.

Fast forward to what we just read in 1 Corinthians Chapters 3 and 6 and remember that we have been given the Holy Spirit of God to indwell us, right? Please stay with me...

Because the Spirit of God was given to us to dwell with us and shall be in us (John 14:17), does that mean that all those ugly-acting, evil spirits that we saw in the first couple chapters of this book, that can live and do dwell in us and **in our flesh** (Romans 7:17-20, Luke 11:24-26, Luke 8:26, Acts 16:16, Mark 9:25, Luke 4:33) automatically left us? I submit to you: **of course not!**

Realize the key: Paul said that "stuff" dwells in him, that is, **in his flesh**. **That's not "the same floor", or "section", of the Temple, where the Holy Spirit dwells.**

What I submit to you is that, now that the Holy Spirit of God has come to dwell in us, we have a lot of "house cleaning to do"...**in the rest of the Temple!**

But Don't Spirits Leave a Person When the Holy Spirit Comes to Indwell the Believer?

Now some of you may have been indoctrinated into a false sense of security in being told that "a Christian cannot have evil spirits". Please realize that Scripture never said it was impossible to have a spirit remain after conversion. And, as a pastor asks right back, "a better question may be 'can an evil spirit have a Christian' "?

Some argue and have been taught that "*evil spirits can't remain when the Holy Spirit comes in.*" If that was so, then there should be no one and nothing left in us that "is sinful" or "wants to sin", and yet we do. And, as we saw and are still seeing, it is **not just** "**the (dead) flesh**".

One answer to the whole dilemma of a believer that has the Holy Spirit also having evil spirits is simple: they do not dwell or reside in the same place or **section** of the temple! Whoever assumed that they would? The Holy Spirit is in the Holy of Holies...and the unclean spirits can reside in the flesh...or outer courts, or atriums.

Since <u>we</u> are the Temple of God, then I submit to you that **we also** have an **Outer Court**, an **Inner Court** and a **Holy of Holies**, just like the Tabernacle of God in the desert that Moses built according to God's pattern and directions, just like the first Temple of God that Solomon built according to God's pattern and directions and just like the second Temple, rebuilt by Ezra and Nehemiah, refurbished and referred to as Herod's Temple in Jesus' times. And, according to God's pattern of the Tabernacle and the Temple...**where exactly was the presence of God?** That's right: **in the Holy of Holies.**

Therefore, I submit to you that the Spirit of God, given to us and which now makes us the Temple of God and the Temple of the Holy Spirit (1 Corinthians 3:16 and 6:19) **resides not in the flesh where the sin of the flesh can reside, where Paul says that dwells no good thing** (Romans 7:18) but rather <u>in the same place where God's presence resided in the previous non-living Temples</u>: in the Holy of Holies.

Do you see? But if you still don't think that you and I can have spirits enter us, ***especially if we "invite them in" or allow them to remain*** (at a different "floor") after the Holy Spirit of God enters us (into our "belly"), then please read on for the revelations and understanding that we've been anticipating all this time, which are the key to **becoming free from the hidden presence *and* influence of the enemy and his spirits in our lives.**

The Fruit of the Spirit Versus the Works of the Flesh

This last section will make the clearest contrast between the Holy Spirit working through us <u>and other spirits working through us</u> and "pulling our strings", which demonstrates the situation and the insights clearly.

Jesus said that you would know them by their fruits.

> **Matthew 7:16 Ye shall know them by their fruits. Do men gather grapes of thorns, or figs of thistles?**
> **17 Even so every good tree bringeth forth good fruit; but a corrupt tree bringeth forth evil fruit.**
> **18 A good tree cannot bring forth evil fruit, neither [can] a corrupt tree bring forth good fruit.**
> **19 Every tree that bringeth not forth good fruit is hewn down, and cast into the fire.**
> **20 Wherefore by their fruits ye shall know them.**

Now let us see what the fruit of the Spirit is:

> **Galatians 5:22 But the fruit of the Spirit is love, joy, peace, longsuffering, gentleness, goodness, faith,**
> **23 Meekness, temperance: against such there is no law.**

So, if we have the Spirit, shouldn't we be manifesting that fruit? Yes, we should. And we do. Therefore, we should not be bringing forth evil fruit, right? **And yet we do**. If we are a good tree, how can we also bring forth evil fruit sometimes? Or are we a corrupt tree?

This is a truth. It is also a parable. The thing is that **people do not "*always* bring *only* good fruit" or "*always* bring *only* bad fruit"**.

The fact is we "good people" or "believers" also sometimes manifest, **temporarily**, "bad fruit"… and so we **also** manifest the "works of the flesh".

> **Galatians 5:19 Now the works of the flesh are manifest, which are [these]; Adultery, fornication, uncleanness, lasciviousness,**
> **20 Idolatry, witchcraft, hatred, variance, emulations, wrath, strife, seditions, heresies,**
> **21 Envyings, murders, drunkenness, revellings, and such like: of the which I tell you before, as I have also told [you] in time past, that they which do such things shall not inherit the kingdom of God.**

You may have wondered, and may be now wondering, what I also wondered. I wondered *why* it is that **sometimes** I would exhibit the fruit of the Spirit but at other times I would also exhibit the works of the flesh.

I had been told by someone very early on in my walk with the Lord that Paul was teaching us that even he himself "could not **help himself**" from sinning, that he himself "could not **control himself**", that he **could not control his sin** or his "flesh" *and therefore* (careful with "therefore's") Paul was teaching that we probably would always have some sins that we would not be able to control and therefore (another one) we might as well let ourselves come to terms with, and accept the fact that, we **could never really, decisively defeat those sins,** and therefore, needed to allow some of those sins, as long as we didn't "habitually practice" those sins. After all, they say, "there is therefore now no condemnation" (alluding to Romans 8:1).

Those conclusions always bothered me because I could not reconcile that with the many other Scriptures that call for, and seem to imply that we **can achieve,** and are supposed to **strive for, holiness** and to **put off** also **"things"** like *anger, wrath, malice*, etc. (Colossians 3:8-9), to **be holy for He is holy** (Leviticus 11:44-45, 19:2; 20:7, 26; 1 Peter 1:14-16; Hebrews 12:14), mortify your mortal members (the flesh!) with its desires and lusts (Galatians 5:24), plus others that warn to not defile and to keep clean the Temple of God, like the two Scriptures we read earlier about us being the Temple of the Holy Spirit.

What I finally saw in Romans 7:17-20 **was *the separation* that Paul was actually making** between **himself** and **the sin that dwelled in his flesh and actually did the sin**! As we made clear in the first two chapters of this book, the sin Paul talks about was **not a thing**, it's **someone** who was **alive** and **that someone was separate from Paul** and **that someone** was doing (**implies a will to act**) the sin that Paul did not will nor want to do. So, this was "another spirit being" and so it wasn't really "Paul's own biological or psychological **defect**". And suddenly I also saw why he could not control "**that other someone**".

Let me put it to you this way. Can **you** control **me**? Can **I** control **you**? Can we control anyone *else* besides ourselves? We might try to manipulate or control each other and we often do that pretty well, but ultimately **you** cannot **convince me** to drink something if I really decide not to. Nor can I keep you from eating something if you really want to and simply decide to. Why? Because **you are not me** and **I am not you** and we are **different and separate people**! We are **two different beings; two different persons**.

It is the same with Paul and "his" sin and me and "my" sin. Paul and I cannot **convince the will, or desires, or urges**, of this sin **being**. Get it? So, do we allow it and condone it? <u>Do we just blame it? No. God forbid</u>. What then? Reckon ourselves helpless?

Oh child of God, do you not **see the simple "third alternative"? Yes, there is another choice; there is another possibility. It is so obvious that I wonder how I never saw it before!**

Isn't this how it can be sometimes with something so obvious that we just "didn't think of it"? It is like the riddle: *"What do you read, sit on and write with? A book, a chair and a pen"*. See? The problem is that we make **an assumption about the answer**: that it has to be one thing but it can also be three separate things! <u>The assumption blocks us from seeing the obvious.</u>

This elusive third alternative to the sin problem is like Scripture says in Colossians 3:8: we "put it off"! That's right; we just "put *it* off"; we just "put *it* away". How?

Let's tie it all together now: **we** are **separate from** sin. Sin **dwells** in our flesh and **is alive**. It's **just like a parasite** that might live in our intestines **or bacteria** that might live in the infected wound in our arm. But these are **spirit beings**, remember? **Spirits live and are separate persons...except they don't have a physical body...*which is why they want to use ours!*** They love to use our physical bodies to act out in this physical world. Sin spirits entered the world, remember? (Romans 5:12).

They started using Adam and Eve's bodies and **the spirits' minds and emotions became evident** as *the hosts* **with the physical bodies acted out the desires of, and the wicked natures of, their spiritual** *"guests"*.

Satan is a spirit, right? He has **no physical body**. And yet he **entered** into Judas, **after first putting it in his heart to betray** Jesus (John 13:2, 27), remember? So, according to Scripture, if we yield ourselves to a sin, we become its, or should we say, **his**, servant, *and "host"*.

You may want or need to review the Scriptures we've reviewed so far if you're not seeing it all tie together yet. However, I know some of you have already been seeing the picture since the first couple of chapters, or the last couple of pages, depending on how the Holy Spirit is working on you to reveal these things.

So, in conclusion: how do we get rid of them? How do we get rid of "spiritual parasites"? Well, how did Jesus cast out evil spirits? How did Paul cast them out? How did the seventy do it? (Luke 10:17) That's right: they did it **in Jesus' name** and Jesus did it **by the power of the Holy Spirit: the "finger of God"**!

Do you get it now? Do you see the revelation about true sanctification now? Do you see that it is possible to be cleaner than ever? Holier than ever? **You don't have to, nor can you, control or "convince" these "things"**. They are **not "your personality"**. They are **other persons**; **evil spirits**, to be exact.

You **don't convince them**, you **cast them out**! You don't "argue with 'yourself'" or **"counsel the evil spirit"** in another. We must first REALIZE that *they* are **thinking, feeling, wanting, lusting and desiring in and through you and me**!

And **THEN, in the Name above all names, we can definitely cast *them* out.**

Does all this sound radical or un-Biblical? It shouldn't.

Only One Spirit Has God's Permission to Be in and Manifest Through God's Temple

And now, here's the final and perhaps most powerful revelation that can be coupled with the revelations from the first two chapters.

If my body is the Temple of the Holy Spirit, then according to God's Manual, which I also call my personal "Code of Conduct", **only one Spirit has the Scriptural right and permission from God to dwell and manifest in this temple, and that is *the Holy* Spirit.**

And **since I choose, by my will, to be one with God only**, I realized one day that **I am only supposed to have the thoughts and feelings of the Holy Spirit**. And do you know what are **the "personality characteristics" of the person of the Holy Spirit**, which is **the only Spirit that I now choose to allow to dwell in me and influence me**? The fruit of the Spirit!

> **Galatians 5:22 But the fruit of the Spirit is love, joy, peace, longsuffering, gentleness, goodness, faith,**
> **23 Meekness, temperance: against such there is no law.**

You see, I realized that **those are *the only* thoughts and feelings I am supposed to have**. I am **not supposed to have** *thoughts or feelings of depression, hopelessness, or defeat.* I am also **not supposed to have or allow** thoughts, feelings or desires for *anger, wrath, malice, or for criticizing or accusing others, or find faults, or keep records of wrongs, or feel accused or rejected or unloved or despised.* I am **not supposed to feel, think or have** *the urges for the works of the flesh or any ungodly lusts or addictions.*

I realized that **all that stuff** was alive. **There was an evil spirit that matched each ungodly "characteristic".** They were all **evil spirits of the evil kingdom of the evil one**.

I was taught, and also resolved, to do like Jesus did: **to kick out every person that did not belong in the Temple! I resolved to get rid of every spirit that was not the Holy Spirit! And they all get evicted in Jesus' Name!**

When I resolved to do that, because I realized that was what, or rather, *who* was "feeding me", and thus causing, every ungodly sin I had ever wrestled with, I decided to *stop wrestling with them and trying to control them.* I could not anyway, and now, I realized why! Everything made sense!

I was shown to just identify, then repent, and RENOUNCE them, AND THEN TO, ALSO, cast them out to the dry places! *THAT is "effective warfare".*

Just trying to "stop the sin" or "control the flesh" is not only fruitless; it is also tragically INCOMPLETE and Biblically ignorant. Sorry, but it is true. "Resisting the devil" and his devils is one thing; "resisting my flesh", as if the problem was coming from me ONLY, is what I mean is incomplete and ignorant. And **the enemy wants us to keep trying to fight "ourselves" that way! Why? Because then we never deal with his devils, his kingdom, in and through us!**

God showed it to me this way: if I ever manifest, or act out, any characteristics except those of the Holy Spirit, as listed in Galatians 5:22-23, then it was **a sure sign that I was being affected by** "another spirit". If I'm hearing thoughts and/or feeling emotions and/or wanting to speak, feel and act out those things that are opposite to, or simply are not the fruit of the Spirit, **then almost certainly I am being attacked and approached by "another spirit",** like in the Garden of Eden, **seeking to make me act oppositely to the Word of God**!

If that's the case, I can be sure that it is not the one and only Spirit to whom I want to yield myself, and want to be a servant of, unto righteousness! (Romans 6:16).

> **Romans 6:16 Know ye not, that to whom ye yield yourselves servants to obey, his servants ye are to whom ye obey; whether of sin unto death, or of obedience unto righteousness?**

17 But God be thanked, that ye were the servants of sin, but ye have obeyed from the heart that form of doctrine which was delivered you.

18 Being then made free from sin, ye became the servants of righteousness.

19 I speak after the manner of men because of the infirmity of your flesh: for as ye have yielded your members servants to uncleanness and to iniquity unto iniquity; even so now yield your members servants to righteousness unto holiness.

20 For when ye were the servants of sin, ye were free from righteousness.

21 What fruit had ye then in those things whereof ye are now ashamed? for the end of those things [is] death.

22 But now being made free from sin, and become servants to God, ye have your fruit unto holiness, and the end everlasting life.

Now I am truly able to yield myself to be a steadier servant to God! And as verses 19 and 22 above say, I can now really achieve **holiness**...better than ever before!

Verse 22 makes more sense now. We are **being made** free from sin, but **not "automatically"**, **through** Yeshua HaMashiach; I am free to become a servant of God **through Jesus' authority and the power of the Spirit of God to cast out evil spirits and to keep them out and tell them to "get thee behind me"**.

Do you see? Realizing that **I am fighting "persons" makes all the difference** and **now I see the enemy**! Before, **I tried to wrestle with emotions and thoughts**...all the while **the persons, whose thoughts and emotions those were, remained hidden and stayed "in my**

Temple"! No wonder I was "up and down" and "only up temporarily". Oh, what a wretched man that I was! (Romans 7:24) I also cried out like Paul until I realized how to have **a real, lasting victory**.

Praises, blessing, honor, glory and power be unto God for bringing these revelations of His Truth and of what He provided, that I may be truly able to get free from sin, remove sin and **fight a more effective battle with the real enemies**, who have now been revealed and identified. I now know about the enemies that I'm fighting...and **it was not just "*myself*"**. Praise God!

And that, my brothers and sisters in the Messiah, is what I have been leading up to all this time.

We have to recognize the difference between "us" and "them" working through us, pushing us, influencing us and "pulling our strings".

But now, there's even more.

Now that we know this, let us take **a closer look at how these "illegal intruders in our Temple" affect our lives when they are hidden and are not removed**.

You'll be amazed at how much stuff that happens in our lives is suddenly and clearly **not the work of the Holy Spirit**...but **the work of "another spirit"**.

And, **once we identify the activity and presence** of those "things" (evil, invisible spirit beings), **we can then go on to their removal.**

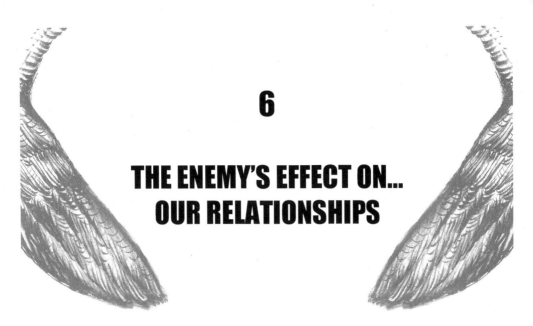

6

THE ENEMY'S EFFECT ON...
OUR RELATIONSHIPS

In the last chapter, we focused on one key "ingredient" from God's Master Plan, the Word of God, which is designed to help us be victorious in our lives and in our battle with the real enemy and his army: that "ingredient" is the person of the Holy Spirit. We looked briefly at why He is a crucial part of our walk and our victory if we are going to be successful.

We then finished the chapter by zeroing in on **His personality and His fruit** so as to identify <u>if it is He who is working through us</u>, as **the only person** inside our temples, <u>or</u> if there might be **other spirits** working **through us** besides, and **in addition to**, **the Holy Spirit**.

Now that we have looked closer at differentiating the Holy Spirit from any other spirit, these next few chapters will focus on recognizing the presence of other spirits in our lives and the devastating effects that are often the result of having these evil spirits **work in our lives and not even realize it** most of the time. As stated in the introduction to this book, much of what the enemy does in our lives happens because **we still largely do not recognize the enemy's**

presence, for he is **largely hidden, unrecognized and not dealt with effectively.**

In this chapter, we will focus in particular on how the enemy and his army devastate our **personal relationships**: friendships, work relationships on the job and in the ministry and especially relationships in the family. We will also note that **marriages are a key target** of the enemy and are being tremendously damaged through the dynamics explained and the examples given in this chapter.

The Enemy's Effect Upon Relationships in General

As stated earlier, the Word of God is God's Master Plan for us and we've agreed that in order to be successful, whether in our personal lives or in any battle against the enemy and his army, we must follow **God's plan and procedures**. His Word is our "Instruction Manual".

His Instruction Manual has much to say about how we ought to get along with one another. We ought to love one another, be patient, kind, forbearing, forgiving and have unity and harmony among us. This is to be present in our personal, family and work relationships. And yet, **the opposite is too often true among the people of God.** Why?

I submit to you that it is **because we have other spirits, *besides the Holy Spirit*, working in our midst and operating *in* and *through* us**. But how can this be?

We have already been exploring how **thoughts and feelings** do not come from dead things nor from only our "flesh", but **from intelligent beings** that **teach us to think, feel and act, with their thoughts, feelings and emotions,** and can also be hidden in us, who are supposed to be the temples of the Holy Spirit (1 Corinthians 3:16, 6:19). We've seen that **the real problem** is "the **sin** that **dwells** in the **flesh"** and that **sin does the sin** that we do not want to do. **Sin is the act** that we do not want to do *but it is also the being that does the act* (Romans 7:17-20) through us and makes us think and feel that it is right to do so.

We saw in the last chapter that the Person of Holy Spirit has a **personality** that is **described as His fruit**. His fruit means that the result of His presence is having these characteristics in us and that when it is He that is "acting through us", or teaching us to learn to act that way, we should see that fruit.

> **Galatians 5:22 But the fruit of the Spirit is love, joy, peace, longsuffering, gentleness, goodness, faith,**
> **23 Meekness, temperance: against such there is no law.**

Again, **let us see the contrast** shown to us **in our Instruction Manual** between the fruit of the Spirit and the works of the flesh:

> **Galatians 5:19 Now the works of the flesh are manifest, which are [these]; Adultery, fornication, uncleanness, lasciviousness,**
> **20 Idolatry, witchcraft, hatred, variance, emulations, wrath, strife, seditions, heresies,**
> **21 Envyings, murders, drunkenness, revellings, and such like: of the which I tell you before, as I have also told [you] in time past, that they which**

do such things shall not inherit the kingdom of God.

This is what we may have never realized before: could it be said that such fruit as that named above could ever be <u>motivated or driven by the Holy Spirit of God</u>? **Of course not.**

The problem is that, until now, **many have attributed these acts**, which are the result of thoughts and feelings, **solely to the physical persons** doing those sins. Though the persons often struggle with these sinful thoughts and feelings and do not want to do those sinful acts, <u>the person is still blamed as being the</u> **sole creator, cause and source** of those thoughts, feelings and acts.

But, what if, as stated before, these unholy thoughts and feelings come upon mankind, at a given point in time, **from un-holy spirits**, in much the same way that God's thoughts and feelings come to us **from the Holy Spirit** of God? We sometimes accept, agree with and act out God's thoughts and feelings and act in accordance with God's Word, our "Code of Conduct". Other times, we accept, agree with and act out un-godly thoughts and feelings which are in disobedience with God's Word and are in accordance with the enemy's desire for us. <u>Does it not stand to reason that it is he and his army *exerting their influence*, in thoughts and feelings? But we do not realize that these come from un-holy spirits</u>. Remember *"Radio God and Radio Devil"*?

We see then that we are **ever having to choose** between going along, in thought, feeling, word and deed, **either with God** and His Word and His "Code of Conduct", **or**, **with some other way**. Do we not see that any influence to think, feel, speak or act in **any other way** other than God's way **does not come from God?** And if so, it comes from the enemy and his army.

And we also must somehow learn **to not be carried away by the influence of these enemies** and **to not accept** those influences **as our own way of thinking, feeling, speaking or acting**.

If we do, we will instantly be "out of compliance" with God's Laws, "Rules and Regulations", "Policies and Procedures": in other words, we have **obeyed other spirits instead of** the Holy Spirit. We will manifest the works of the flesh (of the **sin beings that are "the flesh"** and do the sin) instead of the fruit of the Spirit, of Whom we are supposed to be led by.

> **Romans 8:14 For as many as are led by the Spirit of God, they are the sons of God.**
>
> **Romans 8:1 [There is] therefore now no condemnation to them which are in Christ Jesus, who walk not after the flesh, but after the Spirit.**

Therefore, we see that all acts in our relationships that can be described as dealing unkindly, deceitfully, impatiently, angrily, etc. **are not motivated by the Holy Spirit**. They are motivated by **other spirits**. **Spirits of *hatred, anger, jealousy, bitterness, resentment and unforgiveness*** that taint our personal, work, ministry and family relationships to the point that the results are dissensions, strife, division, fights and even violence. **Everything**, from peace, love and harmony to productivity, achieving success and completing any tasks or objectives, **is disrupted.**

This is the tragic result when we fail to reject the enemy's influence **and go along with those "ungodly procedures"** instead of the Godly procedures outlined in His Word and motivated by the Holy Spirit.

Blaming ONLY Each Other in Our Relationships

The first reason that the above occurs and results is because **people are blaming people**! **Physical**, flesh-and-blood believers are **ONLY blaming** other **physical believers** *as if we were ONLY wrestling against flesh and blood*...but Scripture tells us that this is absolutely not the case!

This truth is **basic** in our "combat Manual" **and yet we seem to be forgetting it every time someone commits a "foul" against another!**

Have we already forgotten the Scripture below, with which we started our study? **We must not:**

> **Ephesians 6:12: For we wrestle not against flesh and blood, but against principalities, against powers, against the rulers of the darkness of this world, against spiritual wickedness in high [places].**

This Scripture is essential to remember in our daily walk. If we do, as well as the principles and revelations we have gleaned so far from this study, we will begin to see the relatively **simple solution to solving and healing the rifts in the Body of Messiah**.

In Chapter 1, we briefly discussed how a person could receive thoughts and feelings from a spirit of anger and end up being **influenced** by it into acting out that anger or violence against that other person that supposedly "did something wrong".

We must realize that **such is always the pattern**: **the enemy and his army** is composed of **spirits such as fear, worry, anxiety, *jealousy, envy, accusation, bitterness, resentment, unforgiveness, retaliation, anger, hatred, violence, murder*,** etc. It is **these spirits** that **cause believers**, just as they cause the unbelievers, **to feel those feelings and think the thoughts that fuel and justify those feelings**. Then, **the person affected** by these spirits **believes "it is true"** that whatever they are feeling or thinking is really that way. Then, they are led to start strife and conflict because of the perceived "problem" or trespass committed against them!

On the other end, there are also **spirits of *rejection, depression, discouragement, sadness, grief, sorrow, and feeling unloved,*** etc. that then come upon those that "get jumped on" by those mentioned above or afflict and oppress those that perceive apparent trespasses, injustices or "unfair" circumstances.

The result is that these believers end up processing everything **as if they were just dealing with physical people in physical circumstances** and end up feeling, thinking, speaking and acting in agreement with **all kinds of spirits besides** the Holy Spirit! And, as we learned from Scripture, **when** we do that, **it becomes our sin,** as we yield ourselves to sin and become one with the sin beings and thus, their servants:

> Romans 6:16 Know ye not, that *to whom ye yield yourselves servants to obey, his servants ye are to whom ye obey; whether of sin* unto death, or of obedience unto righteousness?

This then becomes the sin that dwells in the flesh, that does the sin that we do not want to do. Thus, they've entered into us...to continue their influence again and again, robbing us of our abundant life. Tragic, isn't it?

By not discerning that we wrestle evil spirits that are influencing our brothers and sisters in Messiah, we end up getting caught in a **cycle of "responding in kind",** which, **according to our Manual, we are not supposed to do.**

> Matthew 5:44 But I say unto you, Love your enemies, bless them that curse you, do good to them that hate you, and pray for them which despitefully use you, and persecute you;
> 45 That ye may be the children of your Father which is in heaven: for he maketh his sun to rise on the evil and on the good, and sendeth rain on the just and on the unjust.
> 46 For if ye love them which love you, what reward have ye? do not even the publicans the same?
> 47 And if ye salute your brethren only, what do ye more [than others]? do not even the publicans so?
> 48 Be ye therefore perfect, even as your Father which is in heaven is perfect.

> James 3:9 Therewith bless we God, even the Father; and therewith curse we men, which are made after the similitude of God.

10 Out of the same mouth proceedeth blessing and cursing. My brethren, <u>these things ought not so to be</u>.

1 Thessalonians 5:15 See that <u>none render evil for evil</u> unto any [man]; but ever follow that which is good, both among yourselves, and to all [men].

1 Peter 3:8 Finally, [be ye] all of one mind, having compassion one of another, love as brethren, [be] pitiful, [be] courteous:
9 Not <u>rendering evil for evil, or railing for railing: but contrariwise blessing</u>; knowing that ye are <u>thereunto called</u>, that ye should inherit a blessing.

According to our Manual, we are to react oppositely in many ways. Though we may know this, all too often **we do not act as we are commanded to act because we also fail to discern that what we feel and think** is **coming from hidden spirits!** Therefore, the bitterness, resentment and unforgiveness we feel lead us to believe that these are "true", instead of His Truth (John 17:17) and thus, we **accept them** and **act them out!**

Do you see that this is <u>our deception</u>? And do you see how that deception **causes us to wreck our relationships**?

I am not just talking about "what not to do". I am talking about "stopping it" by recognizing and casting <u>them</u> out. Recognize the spiritual beings causing the "improper behavior" and cast them out. **When *they* are gone, so is *their influence*: their thoughts, feelings, desires and urges to act sinfully!**

The Enemy's Effect Upon Relationships in the Workplace

The spirits of the enemy that have been mentioned, as well as many others, wreak havoc in the **work relationships** also. While God created man to subdue the earth and take dominion over it and the animals, **the spiritual enemies we battle** have led us to seek instead to subdue and take dominion over each other!

Nations and regimes seek to dominate and control other peoples and do so through oppression, violence and all manner of evil works. Certainly such evil and contradictions do not originate nor are motivated by the Holy Spirit of God. Greed also drives otherwise peaceful (non-violent) men to seek to defraud, lie and cheat in order to achieve monetary gain, usually at the expense of others. This has become the norm for far too many people upon this earth and is a direct result of not walking in accordance with our Maker's Manual. And that is a result of **being counseled, led, spoken to and made to feel and think by spirits** of all manner of greed, wickedness and unrighteousness.

And, not only have these "things" driven the work environment itself, but the personal relationships in the workplace are affected by all these as well. **People are being hurt and wounded in the workplace every day!** Even in work environments where "direct evil" is not practiced, spirits of *accusation, anger, resentment, unforgiveness, retaliation*, etc. cause many to **mistreat others** who, in turn, come under the attack of spirits that cause all manner of thoughts and feelings of *insecurity, fear, torment, depression, helplessness, defeat, grief, sorrow, rejection*, etc.

Therefore, instead of man working together with man in a friendly environment that fosters cooperation and synergy, the result is an environment of hostility, fear and self-preservation. Such is not conducive to people reaching contentment and satisfaction; instead, it often becomes a place **where the enemy works greatly at tormenting and hurting people** through lies, mistreatment, abuse and all manner of situation where **people are not loving one another as we are commanded by our Maker**. We neither receive love nor do we love others.

> **Leviticus 19:18 Thou shalt not avenge, nor bear any grudge against the children of thy people, but thou shalt love thy neighbour as thyself: I [am] the LORD.**

> **Zechariah 8:17 And let none of you imagine evil in your hearts against his neighbour; and love no false oath: for all these [are things] that I hate, saith the LORD.**

> **Matthew 22:37 Jesus said unto him, Thou shalt love the Lord thy God with all thy heart, and with all thy soul, and with all thy mind.**
> **38 This is the first and great commandment.**
> **39 And the second [is] like unto it, Thou shalt love thy neighbour as thyself.**
> **40 On these two commandments hang all the law and the prophets.**

Spirits of *insecurity, suspicion, hatred, resentment, jealousy and envy*, for example, ruin the relationships between managers and the workers they manage. Managers often are *afraid* of others taking their positions, so they do not help their workers to improve and grow: they stifle them instead and "keep them down". Those workers, in turn, *resent* such treatment and <u>then seek to do the very thing the managers sought to prevent. At the end of the day, everyone hates and resents each other and when they go home, hurt, rejection, sadness, depression and hopelessness reign.</u>

This then even spills into other relationships, such as the family dynamics in **marriages** and **between parents and children.**

Are you getting the picture?

The Enemy's Effect Upon Relationships in the Ministry

The enemy's attacks against the Body of Messiah at large are bad enough. One would think that those in what is commonly referred to as "the ministry", or those in leadership in the Body of Messiah, would be less susceptible to the attacks of the enemy normally found in those in the Body who are not in leadership or ministry positions. Sadly, the same ravages that occur in the Body at large **also occur in the ministry...***and perhaps even more so.*

It is perhaps understandable that those in the work of the ministry would be **more of a target for the enemy** than those not in the ministry. After all, these are the people who formally work against the enemy and are more involved in the building of the Kingdom of God on earth, ministering and teaching the people of God and building up the Body of believers. Indeed, these men and women are involved most directly in the organized effort to bring God's plans and purposes to pass here on the earth.

But what would also be expected is that these men and women would be more victorious in their personal and corporate battle against the enemy. After all, if these people are teaching others in the Body, one would expect that these people have learned more on how to be successful in "standing against the wiles of the devil" (Ephesians 6:11-13) and that they are being successful in their personal lives and in their corporate effort in the ministry. While they are certainly not expected to be "perfect", one would expect them to be largely successful and, for the most part, to have reached the point of being largely stable, mature and **at least more discerning**.

> **1 Timothy 3:2 A bishop then must be blameless, the husband of one wife, vigilant, sober, of good behaviour, given to hospitality, apt to teach;**
> **3 Not given to wine, no striker, not greedy of filthy lucre; but patient, not a brawler, not covetous;**
> **4 One that ruleth well his own house, having his children in subjection with all gravity;**
> **5 (For if a man know not how to rule his own house, how shall he take care of the church of God?)**
> **6 Not a novice, lest being lifted up with pride he fall into the condemnation of the devil.**
> **7 Moreover he must have a good report of them which are without; lest he fall into reproach and the snare of the devil.**
> **8 Likewise [must] the deacons [be] grave, not doubletongued, not given to much wine, not greedy of filthy lucre;**
> **9 Holding the mystery of the faith in a pure conscience.**
> **10 And let these also first be proved; then let them use the office of a deacon, being [found] blameless.**

11 Even so [must their] wives [be] grave, not slanderers, sober, faithful in all things.

12 Let the deacons be the husbands of one wife, ruling their children and their own houses well.

Titus 1:7 For a bishop must be blameless, as the steward of God; not selfwilled, not soon angry, not given to wine, no striker, not given to filthy lucre;

8 But a lover of hospitality, a lover of good men, sober, just, holy, temperate;

9 Holding fast the faithful word as he hath been taught, that he may be able by sound doctrine both to exhort and to convince the gainsayers.

Titus 2:2 That the aged men be sober, grave, temperate, sound in faith, in charity, in patience.

3 The aged women likewise, that [they be] in behaviour as becometh holiness, not false accusers, not given to much wine, teachers of good things;

4 That they may teach the young women to be sober, to love their husbands, to love their children,

5 [To be] discreet, chaste, keepers at home, good, obedient to their own husbands, that the word of God be not blasphemed.

The above are just some of the qualities that, according to the Word of God, are expected to be found among those in leadership in the Body. The point being made is **neither for accusation or condemnation** of anyone who presently fails or has in the past failed in any of these areas, for I myself have failed miserably, and everyone fails sometimes. The point, as stated in the introduction, is that there is a serious problem in the Body of Messiah in that we are not exactly displaying victorious lives over the enemy. The point being made is simply that even the leadership, those expected to be more mature, solid and stable than those in the Body at large, are often **not any more discerning**, and thus, no more "compliant with Scriptural standards", than the rest of the Body. Therefore, we are not achieving what can be achieved.

As I personally found out through my own failures, the point being made in this book is that **there is <u>a</u> <u>little-known yet powerful solution</u> to the serious problems** in the Body of Messiah and that **the solution comes from first recognizing the real problem: that it is not just "us"...<u>but it is the</u> <u>enemy and his army that is hidden and</u> <u>operating...even amongst ourselves</u>.**

As stated in the previous section, **<u>the pattern</u> is** always the same: **various spirits, *whose fruit is opposite that of the Holy Spirit's*, influence us through their thoughts and feelings, then we believe that those thoughts and feelings "prove" that what we feel and think is "true" and then we act accordingly, even though the acts are in direct contradiction and disobedience to our "Code of Conduct".** It almost seems that we are helpless to "resist".

And indeed, because of the purpose and work of those in leadership and in the ministry, the enemy attacks these people more deliberately and diligently. And sadly, the enemy and his army continue to enjoy a great deal of success, far too much in fact. And this is why the Spirit of God has prompted and commanded this book, among other people in similar efforts: **<u>to</u> <u>expose and identify the real enemy and his army</u>,** that we may **fight THEM, instead of ourselves or others**, and **then remove them effectively** and finally **walk in victory**.

Some Common Attacks and Effects on the Ministry

Perhaps the favorite weapon directed at those in the ministry in general involves **contention, division, envying and strife**. It would seem that the enemy relies heavily on the concept "divide and conquer". If he can cause division, **not only does he greatly hinder the Body from accomplishing anything**, he also goes directly against one of the Messiah's greatest prayers and objectives of God: **unity**.

> **John 17:20 Neither pray I for these alone, but for them also which shall believe on me through their word;**
> **21 That they all may be one; as thou, Father, [art] in me, and I in thee, that they also may be one in us: that the world may believe that thou hast sent me.**

By attacking and hindering the objective of unity, the enemy also seeks to prevent its intended result: that the world may believe that Messiah came. Indeed, many unbelievers claim that they cannot or do not believe in the Messiah because the believers are so divided into so many different "camps" and are even divided within their own "groups". We all then get accused of being "hypocrites" and full of hate.

God also speaks of how important **unity** is to Him through King David:

> **Psalms 133:1 Behold, how good and how pleasant [it is] for brethren to dwell together in unity!**
> **2 [It is] like the precious ointment upon the head, that ran down upon the beard, [even] Aaron's**

beard: that went down to the skirts of his garments;
3 As the dew of Hermon, [and as the dew] that descended upon the mountains of Zion: for there the LORD commanded the blessing, [even] life for evermore.

It is said that the enemy knows the Word better than some believers. Indeed he also seems very aware of another Scripture in order to cause a lot of havoc by simply causing **strife**:

James 3:16 For where envying and strife [is], there [is] confusion and every evil work.

Here we see just how far-reaching and effective it is, according to the Word of God, for the enemy to sow and cause envying and strife: **it results, per God's Word, in confusion and just about any and every evil work.** No wonder **strife is so devastating**!

The enemy often causes strife simply by loosing spirits of *criticism, fault-finding and accusation* upon the members of congregations. They speak thoughts of *accusation and criticism* against the pastors and leadership in the ears and minds of unsuspecting members, and loose feelings of *anger, bitterness, offense*, etc. Then, those members believe that they are sensing truths and are deceived into attacking the leaders and sowing discord among other members. They spread their "insights and conclusions" with others, unwittingly opening the doors to other spirits and often increase the intensity and the evil intent **until they often confront and attack the leaders, believing that they are "trying to help" to "correct a wrong".**

Once they do, they are actually directing the **words, thoughts, feelings** and in reality, the "fiery darts of the wicked" (Ephesians 6:16), **which are actually evil spirits**, against the leaders they accost and attack. Sadly, the people are often unaware that they are **being used as conduits by these evil spirits**.

And then, when the **leaders** receive these attacks, **they also often fail to discern what is really happening**, so they actually "receive" these spirits when they are overcome by **thoughts and feelings (spirits)** of *offense, accusation, rejection*, etc. Instead of realizing that they are not wrestling with flesh and blood, **they accept the spirits' influence to "blame the physical people"** and now receive and hold *bitterness, unforgiveness, resentment and anger* against those people and even become *suspicious* and *distrusting* of others who later on may voice dissenting opinions not voiced with evil intent or motivations!

This makes many **leaders** act in direct contradiction to 1 Corinthians 13, which commands (among many things) to think the best and not keep a record of wrongs. They can also become quick to fear another attack and become *defensive, impatient, unloving* and also quick to "attack perceived attacks".

Do you see this scenario? Have you not seen it or experienced it yourself? Sadly, this scenario is far too common and widespread in the Body of Messiah and **it is hindering and even halting the blessings of God**. After all, **if there's envying and strife**, and then there's **confusion and every evil work, how much can love and blessing** *also* **exist in the same environment?** Also, **how much can God bless those**

who are acting in such disobedience to His "Code of Conduct"? Would His **love, blessing, and presence** not be **diluted, diminished and/or compromised**?

The above scenario is particularly devastating **among leaders themselves**. In attempting to work together, differences and challenges can quickly arise. The problem is not the differences or challenges themselves. The problem comes when the leaders **also do not recognize that evil spirits are influencing them to "react in ungodly manners"** rather than to **act by the leading and guidance and control of the Holy Spirit**.

And so, as stated before as the "pattern of the enemy", these **leaders** find themselves thinking and feeling the thoughts and feelings of various evil spirits**,** **believe that these are their own**, and **that they are "true and accurate"**, often *even believing that they are being led of the Holy Spirit*, and then find themselves speaking and acting in fruit that is definitely not that of the Holy Spirit, yet helpless to stop themselves!

The Possibilities are Endless

Sadly, the possibilities for spreading havoc among the leaders in the ministry are almost endless, and perhaps even greater than among the rest of the believers. After all, there are positions, privileges, reputations, prestige, honors, egos and even monetary gain at stake, right? In many ways, it is no different than a secular business or corporation. And again, these sad scenarios are all a result of believers not discerning that they are being made to fight and contend by evil spirits.

As long as we continue to not discern and realize that we are not fighting "mean people", we will continue to not only **receive and not quench** the fiery darts of the enemy, which hurt and wound us spiritually and emotionally, but **we will also continue to "retaliate" and harm in return**, not only those that commit offenses against us, but **also others who later on simply resemble the acts or words of those that have hurt us before**! Thus, we actually "spread the disease" unto others. But this scenario is even worse, for we do not just spread a physical disease; we spread a spiritual contamination of evil spirits.

We all have heard the refrain *"hurt people hurt people"*. This holds true with people who have been hurt and attacked by evil spirits. They do not realize that they often have become "**carriers**" of "things" like **bitterness, resentment, anger, hatred**, etc. Only thing is that these "things" are **not things at all: they are evil spirits**. And **those spirits attack others, through us, often even without our being aware of them or being able to control it or them**!

As I've personally come to realize, and say often since 2005, *"one does not have to be rolling on the floor and foaming at the mouth to have an evil spirit"*. All one has to do is to be in agreement with the thoughts, feelings and words that contradict the Word of God and the fruit of the Holy Spirit and then act in accordance with such. At that point, one is **manifesting the nature of "another spirit"** which is not of God and that is against God and **which is coaching, coaxing, guiding and leading us into disobedience** to the Word and intentions of God.

When these scenarios continue to occur in the ministry, it is no wonder we have the results already noted: **objectives for the Kingdom of God are not accomplished** and **leaders hurt and treat each other,** not in the way the Lord would want, <u>but rather **in the manner that the enemy would like us to**</u> and successfully influences us into doing it...*all the while we don't even think it's him and his army.* <u>**Sadly, we think it's "those sinful people" and their "sinful natures".**</u>

And, as noted before that the spiritual attacks in the workplace can spill over into the family, so also is the case with the spiritual onslaughts that occur in the ministry. **Not only are many leaders hurt terribly themselves, many leaders then unwittingly wound many of the sheep...and/or their own families, spouses and children!** There are many believers that have been hurt, wounded and/or mistreated by leaders in the ministry, further fragmenting the Body of believers. And those wounded people often <u>take those wounds home with them</u> and the evil spirits that infect their spiritual wounds <u>in turn infect and wound their own families.</u>

The Enemy's Effect Upon Relationships in the Family and Home

Lastly, we now come to **the heart of the relationships: the family.** Perhaps this is the enemy's ultimate target. While the ministry is indeed a prime target of the enemy and his army, the family may be even more far-reaching to the enemy's overall plans and objectives to kill, steal and destroy. Why? Because "an ounce of prevention is worth a pound of cure".

In other words, while the enemy is currently having a pretty easy time corrupting people's lives in the workplace and in the ministry, it maybe even easier to hurt, wound, abuse and mistreat mankind while they are still children or even infants! Having seen the pattern of the enemy so far and understanding how he deceives even otherwise mature believers into receiving and spreading evil spirits, perhaps we can now understand how it is **even more destructive to attack and hurt children** through things that are not even necessarily physical! **Studies have shown that emotional and verbal abuse are just as painful, and register the same in the brain, as physical abuse**. Studies have also shown how detrimental it is to mental and emotional health, growth and development when babies and/or children are not loved, held or touched properly. **Just think of how devastating it is then for children to be treated with anger, wrath, hostility, humiliation, denigration and strife**.

The family home is supposed to be the "place of safety" from the rest of the world, in which "strangers" often can be unloving and unkind. And yet, the "home" is often the place where children are yelled at, humiliated and even abused the most, in many terrible ways, before they even have a chance to develop a proper sense of love, value and life!

From the enemy's perspective, it is more effective to mess up a child's life through having its own family members mistreat and afflict them. And yet remember, it is not ultimately the family members that do it: **it is the horde of evil spirits**, such as *rejection, accusation, guilt, bitterness, anger, hatred, criticism, mocking and unloving spirits*, *working through* **the family members**, who themselves were likely also attacked by people through whom those spirits flowed into their lives in the first place.

Some Common Attacks and Effects on the Family and Home

By now, it should not be too hard for you to understand the examples that are being discussed. In fact, by now you are probably beginning to see the same "pattern of the enemy" borne out in many of your own life experiences, whether in the street, the school, the workplace, even the church, congregation...or in your own family. Many of us have had experiences similar to those presented thus far. As we discuss some common examples, it all becomes clearer and we start to see our situations more clearly and with more understanding (it is always the Holy Spirit Who brings us **"revelation about the information"**). Let us now look at some specific examples of how the enemy works in the home and against the family.

"The Giver" and "The Receiver"

I have come to realize, and often say, that the enemy and his army "work on both sides of the fence"; that is to say, they work against both what I call "the giver" and also on "the receiver". "*__The giver__*" is **the first person that is influenced or attacked by the evil spirits** and then acts out ungodly words, attitudes and/or actions against another person, who is "*__the receiver__*" of those words, attitudes or actions. Once the giver acts against the receiver, **then the receiver is also attacked and influenced by another set of evil spirits**, which give their perspective, thoughts and corresponding emotions to the receiver about what is being done or said to them, in reality or in perception.

Example #1: Husband Against Wife

For example, a common attack is for a husband to feel **unloved, rejected, jealous and angry**. As we have learned, this is evidence that **spirits** are **making that man feel unloved, rejected, then jealous and angry** as well as giving him the **"matching thoughts" which make him think that "he's right"** about his situation.

For example, a man's wife went to look for work to help the family's economic situation. When a male friend of both mentioned to the husband that he had seen his wife on the street, the husband became overwhelmed with thoughts of an affair between the two and became convinced that such was the case. Being convinced by "the logic" as well as being carried away by his feelings of jealousy, anger and being unloved, he then began to accuse his wife and fight with her, becoming more and more enraged, as she denied the situation, eventually becoming violent. The husband in this example is obviously "the giver", as he is giving the unkind treatment to the wife, who is then "the receiver".

Well, now the enemy went to work <u>also</u> on the wife. As the receiver of ill treatment, accusations, anger, unloving words and the treatment that culminated in violence, evil **spirits *of fear, torment, accusation, rejection, anger, hatred, bitterness, resentment and also feeling unloved*** went to work <u>on her</u>. They flooded her with **thoughts about** how bad the situation is and how badly she was being treated, and falsely at that.

Notice that **some of these spirits are common to her husband and are in fact, coming through him** (spirits of **rejection, anger and** feelings of **being unloved**) while **others are specially suited to her in her situation as "the receiver"** of the unfair and ungodly treatment (spirits of **fear, torment, accusation, hatred, bitterness** and **resentment**).

Also notice that **the spirits are not "lying"** to the woman about her situation: she **is** being accused, tormented, rejected and not being loved, plus the hostility (that is verbal, emotional and physical) certainly affirms fear. Realize that **spirits do not attack only when there is no truth** in their feelings, thoughts or situations. In fact, **they capitalize on situations that are "true",** in the sense that they are really "happening", **because then the "matching thoughts" are extremely convincing to the person** that they are really under a threat that calls for their own set of ungodly reactions. But, as we have already seen, God expects us to act opposite to improper treatment.

Please know that I absolutely understand the woman in this example. By my stating that the enemy is influencing her, I am not at all condoning him. However, God expects her to not react in an ungodly manner all the while she removes herself from the line of fire if necessary while seeking help for **the man to stop his ungodly thoughts, feelings and acts. He needs deliverance** from these evil spirits, **same as she** does. **Though there is a "giver" and a "receiver",** both **are being afflicted by evil spirits and** both **will need deliverance from these evil**

spirits. They both need Scriptural teaching on this subject. *"Regular" counseling, that does not take the evil spirits into account, will be ineffective at best and useless or counterproductive at worst*, as seen in earlier chapters.

My point is that God has Scriptural guidelines for "the receivers" <u>as well as</u> "the givers". While He certainly does not expect the receivers to simply "allow it and do nothing", He certainly <u>does not expect the receiver to also act and respond un-Scripturally</u>. Even in God's economy, and perhaps especially so, "two wrongs do not make a right".

Having pointed this out, we now see that **evil spirits** went to the husband, **influenced him through thoughts and feelings** about a situation and **"threw him" against** his wife. Once he did that, evil spirits also then went to the wife and **influenced her, also through thoughts and feelings**, and **now both were acting and responding in ungodly and unscriptural ways.**

Thus, **the cycle** has begun and they are both now caught up in a situation full of "confusion and every evil work".

Example #2: Wife Against Husband

Now, let us look at another example, this time where the wife is "the giver".

Let's say there's a woman who had been abused by her stepfather as a child and later by other men since high school and beyond. They had not loved her as

God would have and abused her verbally, emotionally and physically. To cope, she "became tough" while still carrying **spirits** of *bitterness, resentment, anger, hatred, accusation, fear of being controlled and abused further* also within her.

She then married a man who happened to be of a particular ethnic origin. A well-meaning friend of the woman, without knowing this particular man, "warned" her about men of that ethnic group "being known for being controlling". Sounding "factual" to her, this woman "agreed with" this thought and soon, evil spirits of *fear* of being controlled, *anger, resentment, bitterness and accusation* made the woman feel these emotions whenever the couple dealt with various situations as newly-married husband and wife. Even questions about where to have dinner sounded to the woman as efforts on the part of the man to "control her".

Feeling these feelings and having the "matching thoughts" from the accusing mind of the spirits that were accusing him of scheming and exercising an ungodly control, the woman, being led by the spirits and believing fully that things were as they seemed to "her" (to the evil spirits within her and around her), she quickly and often attacked her husband with *anger, accusation, hostility, rejection* and *harsh, unloving* words and ways. Ironically, she felt she was "defending herself" the whole time. In this example, she was "the giver".

Meanwhile, on the "other side of the fence", the husband was being attacked by a whole other set of evil spirits, **in addition to** the ones working through the wife against him. **Spirits** of *feeling unloved, disrespected, accused, hated, suspected,* *misunderstood, thought of badly, mistrusted,* etc. were "having a field day" with him. The more he tried to "explain" and talk and defuse the situation, the more he was mistreated by her **and the spirits** that **yelled at, insulted, demeaned, denigrated and accused him of even worse schemes**. As the pattern continued, the hurts and wounds grew and **spirits** of *depression, grief, sorrow, defeat, hopelessness and even self-destruction* began to attack him, all the while using "the reality" to convince the husband that "all was lost" and that "no solution would ever be found" and that "things would only get worse." Thus, in this episode, the husband was "the receiver".

Again, we see that **strife** and the other spirits have opened the way for "confusion and every evil work".

Fortunately, teaching and deliverance came to this couple and they were able to remove the enemy and be reconciled.

Someone recently said, speaking about the conflict in the Middle East, that if you want two groups of people to fight, all you have to do is convince one of them that they are either in danger or under a threat from the other. I would submit that this example is **applicable to individuals** and would add that one could also simply **convince one that they are being treated unfairly or improperly.** *That alone is also enough to foster ungodly thoughts and feelings* that open the door to many of the evil spirits that we are discussing in these examples.

Example #3: Mother Against Children

Now let us look at an example in which a mother might relate improperly with her children due to the work of evil spirits.

Being a parent is definitely a "tall assignment" and carries with it great demands and pressures. Being a single mother certainly only heightens those demands and pressures. However, though we certainly sympathize with such a one, God's Manual for Life has Truths and Promises that assure us that we can do all things through Messiah and that God does not allow more than we can handle (Philippians 4:13, 1 Corinthians 10:13). Therefore, God's Truths guide such a mother to also be able to do her job **while maintaining God's standards for her conduct**; that is, *as long as evil spirits do not have "the upper hand" or the dominion over her.* **But what if they do?**

For example, let's say a woman was unhappy growing up as a child and as a young woman. Her father often abused her emotionally and verbally as well as her mother and siblings. She also grew up to be rejected and unloved by friends and boys. After she married her first boyfriend, pressures of marriage led to difficulties in which she resorted to verbal abuse, accusation and insults, just as her father had. Though her husband made mistakes and resorted to ungodly escapism, withdrawal and alcohol, she certainly did not make matters better. Spirits of ***resentment*** and ***accusation*** against her husband soon grew to full-blown ***bitterness, anger, hatred***, etc. Soon, the marriage ended with "irreconcilable differences" and he left her for another woman who would treat him "better", adding spirits of ***guilt and self-accusation,*** *self-hatred and self-blame* to her list of evil attackers and evil "passengers" in her "mobile temple". To add insult to injury, the husband left her with a young child and another one in the womb.

This young mother now had two children to raise on her own. Full of the evil spirits named above, her job as single mother is **exponentially harder**. She does not cope well with pressure, loses patience quickly and is prone to become angry, defensive and verbally and emotionally abusive when feeling overwhelmed or "accosted" by her children. Therefore, she often screams to her children in anger when they ask for things or needs of all sorts, voicing her own hopelessness about her own life or even blaming them for the financial difficulties she faces. She is, in this example, "the giver", though she has certainly been "the receiver" since childhood. (Remember the refrain *"hurt people hurt people"*?)

Her children are then being "the receivers". They receive the **words, thoughts and emotions** of these **same evil spirits** that worked **through her father and her ex-husband into her,** and which are still working directly against the mother by giving her thoughts and feelings anytime they want. These spirits constantly seek to manifest their nature through the mother and **when she fails to discern** that these thoughts, feelings and actions **do not come from her alone, nor from the Holy Spirit, but rather from evil spirits** (Ephesians 6:12), **she fails to keep them from acting upon her children, who then "receive" these evil spirits into their temples**. And so, the cycle continues.

The result is that the children feel *rejection, guilt, shame, blame, condemnation* and *being unloved.*

Those spirits come through the mother against them and they do not know how to reject them, for **they do not discern, them either**. In addition, spirits of *bitterness, resentment, unforgiveness, rebellion, anger* and *even depression, sadness, grief, sorrow and hopelessness* also attack them directly as "the receivers" and enter in and dwell in them (Luke 11:26), thus further compounding their problems and causing them **hurt, torment and a very unhappy existence from a very early age.**

The Enemy's Effect Upon Relationships: Final Thoughts

This is but a small sampling of the effect of the enemy's kingdom of evil spirits upon mankind and his relationships in various settings. These effects are perhaps best summed up by the words of the Messiah.

> **John 10:10 The thief cometh not, but for to steal, and to kill, and to destroy: I am come that they might have life, and that they might have [it] more abundantly.**

The enemy and his evil spirits certainly have been very busy, and have been very successful, at doing this in countless workplaces, ministries, homes and families. What makes this reality so ironic is that **God did not leave us at a disadvantage. He furnished us with everything we ever needed to be victorious**, not only in the workplace, ministry and the home and family front but also in the true battlefield. And yet, the reality seen above would seem to contradict the Truths and Promises in God's Word:

2 Peter 1:3 According as his divine power <u>hath given unto us all things that [pertain] unto life and godliness</u>, through the knowledge of him that hath called us to glory and virtue:

Matthew 16:18 And I say also unto thee, That thou art Peter, and upon this rock I will build my church; and <u>the gates of hell shall not prevail against it</u>.

Luke 10:19 Behold, <u>I give unto you power to tread on serpents and scorpions, and over all the power of the enemy: and nothing shall by any means hurt you</u>.

Indeed, He did give us power over the enemy and the gates of hell should not prevail against us. **So, why is the enemy prevailing?**

As stated in the introduction and since, it is **largely because the enemy is hidden, not being discerned** and therefore **not being identified neither as separate from "physical people" nor as the "spiritual enemies" that they are** per Ephesians 6:12.

Therefore, they are going **largely unnoticed and undealt with. They are being "left alone".** *This must stop.*

Jesus paid a very high price to obtain the power and authority, among other things, for us to be able to cast out devils, and then commanded us to go do as He did.

Matthew 10:7 And as ye go, preach, saying, The kingdom of heaven is at hand.

8 Heal the sick, cleanse the lepers, raise the dead, <u>cast out devils</u>: freely ye have received, freely give.

If we do not **recognize, attack and defeat the real enemy** and his army, we will not only see the ravages **in our relationships** continue, but we will also see the same destruction continue in the next area we will look at in the next chapter: the area of our ***obedience, walk, and relationship with God***.

7

THE ENEMY'S EFFECT ON...
OUR WALK AND RELATIONSHIP
WITH YAHWEH

In the last chapter, we looked at how the presence of the enemy and his army in our personal lives affects our relationships with each other. In this chapter, we'll focus on **how the enemy affects us individually** and also **our walk and relationship with God** ("Yahweh" is His "*proper*" or "*specific*" name in Hebrew).

This may be one of the most important chapters of this book because it will show us that **being affected in our walk with God/Yahweh may be costing us almost everything**, and we might not even be aware of it. But I assure you: **our enemy knows exactly what this is costing us**, for it is he (they) doing it to us, on purpose, to sabotage us.

The Enemy Wants to "Short-Circuit" Our Walk with Yahweh

Some might say that the enemy cannot affect our relationship with Yahweh. While the enemy cannot affect or trick Yahweh, he certainly **can** and **does affect and trick *us***. And by affecting *us*, he and his army can **affect our walk with Yahweh**. And our walk with Yahweh determines **our relationship with Him**, which in turn, has a far greater effect than we might imagine. Why? **Because if the enemy affects our relationship with Yahweh, then he affects the very source of everything in our lives**: our power against him, the source of our health, the source of our finances, the source of our peace of mind, our sanity, our blessings...**our very connection to our Source** is affected, hindered, diminished and can even be cut off! **And, if our connection to the Source is cut off, we have nothing! We are left without supply. We are left "separated from Him"**.

Jesus (**Yeshua** in Hebrew) Himself told us: "without Me, you can do nothing".

> **John 15:5 I am the vine, ye [are] the branches: He that abideth in me, and I in him, the same bringeth forth much fruit: for without me ye can do nothing.**
> **6 If a man abide not in me, he is cast forth as a branch, and is withered; and men gather them, and cast [them] into the fire, and they are burned.**
> **7 If ye abide in me, and my words abide in you, ye shall ask what ye will, and it shall be done unto you.**
> **8 Herein is my Father glorified, that ye bear much fruit; so shall ye be my disciples.**
> **9 As the Father hath loved me, so have I loved you: continue ye in my love.**
> **10 If ye keep my commandments, ye shall abide in my love; even as I have kept my Father's commandments, and abide in his love.**

The above verses spell out what happens to us if our walk and relationship with Yahweh is right and if it's not right. And, what happens to us if our walk and relationship with Him are "not right"?

In a nutshell, we wither and we get burned.

Have you ever felt like the rivers of living water stopped flowing and, instead of feeling drenched and moist, you felt parched and dry, as if things simply "don't work out"? I have. And I wondered what had gone wrong.

You know what? I have discovered that the Word of Yahweh is absolutely true in its entirety and the passage above is no exception. Let us look closer and glean some crucial things that may not have been completely clear to us before even though this is another familiar passage of Scripture. Here are some keys worth noting in our continuing study of Yahweh's winning Plan.

1. *If I abide* in Him, I bring forth fruit (verse 5).
2. *If I do not* abide in Him, I <u>wither</u>, men <u>gather me</u> and <u>cast me in the fire</u> and I get burned (verse 6).
3. *If I abide* in Him, I ask and it shall be done unto me (verse 7).
4. *If I keep* His commandments, then I abide in His love, even as Yeshua has kept His Father's commandments and abides in His love (verse 10).

Therefore, we see the aforementioned conclusion at the start of this chapter: without Him we can do nothing. <u>We must stay "right with Him", "connected" and "with access" to Him. But, how exactly do we "get connected" and "stay connected" to Him, our Source?</u> Likewise, **what could "disconnect us"?**

We often know much and are taught much about how to connect with Him...**but there are also things that can hinder our efforts or even nullify and cancel our efforts to connect!** To achieve something, we must not only "do what achieves it" but we must also **not do** the things that could "disqualify us".

> **1 Corinthians 9:27 But I keep under my body, and bring [it] into subjection: lest that by any means, when I have preached to others, I myself should be a castaway.**

Therefore, <u>we must realize that there are "things" that can get us "out of a right standing" with Yahweh</u> and become a castaway after we have preached about Yahweh's ways. Paul refers to his body. What does he mean? I submit to you that he's also talking about that "sin that dwells in the flesh", because, as we have seen by now, **the sin that dwells in the flesh can make us think, feel and act in sinful ways** *if we do not discern, cast out those sin-ners, and keep them from controlling us*.

How Sin in the Flesh Can Ruin Our Walk with Yahweh

It's like scoring a touchdown: much goes into scoring that touchdown and it takes much coaching, effort, and practice to achieve it. But if that player grabbed a face mask on the way to the end zone, it matters little how spectacular a run that player made: **the touchdown is "taken back". He usually also gets a penalty, either individually or for the team**.

It is the same for Yahweh's team on earth. Sometimes we do anything and everything to achieve something for Yahweh. But then, we realize we might have done something "illegal" and so Paul tells us that we might become a castaway. In other words, we ourselves become "disqualified" from the very things we preach.

Do you see it? A football player may not *want* to grab that face mask, or use "unnecessary roughness" when making a winning play, but if he cannot keep from doing that, his winning play will be of none effect and he might even get a penalty for himself and/or his team. **Likewise, a believer may not want to do something "illegal" as he serves the Lord** but if he cannot keep from doing that, *as can be the case when sin does what we do not want to do (Romans 7:20),* then we might ourselves become penalized instead of receiving the full blessings that come from behaving "according to the Rules".

Therefore, the question is: "*what is* 'legal' and 'by the Rules' instead of 'illegal' "?

Jesus (Yeshua) tells us about this in John 15:10; He tells us to "**keep My commandments**". John 15:7 also tells us another way: "**abide in Me** and **My words abide in you**". Therefore, **keeping His commandments and abiding in Him and His Word and having His Word in us** would be what Yahweh calls "legal" **and is what Yeshua said would position us in such a way that we ask and it shall be done for us, and that we bear much fruit**.

> **John 15:5 I am the vine, ye [are] the branches: He that abideth in me, and I in him, the same bringeth forth much fruit: for without me ye can do nothing.**

> **7 If ye abide in me, and my words abide in you, ye shall ask what ye will, <u>and it shall be done unto you.</u>**
> **10 If ye keep my commandments, ye shall abide in my love; even as I have kept my Father's commandments, and abide in his love.**

The above three verses seem to be the "winning method" for playing **the believer's "game" "legally"**, not according to N-F-L rules, but **according to G-O-D rules**. And, verse 6 contains both **the "losing method"** as well as **the "penalty"**:

> **6 If a man abide not in me, he is cast forth as a branch, and is withered; and men gather them, and cast [them] into the fire, and they are burned.**

So there we have it. The Master teaches us that if we do things "His way", according to His Word and commandments, we abide in Him, and in His love, even as He did, **_and then_ we can expect to ask and have it done** unto us and bear much fruit. We "score touchdowns" for Yahweh. And we acknowledge that He is our Coach, through the Holy Spirit (**Ruach HaKodesh** in Hebrew).

But if not, Father "cuts us off" and we wither, dry up and things do not go very well for us. We get "penalties". First, men seem to get the best of us and we fail, instead of us being the blessed of the Lord and being the head and not the tail. Instead, we have all manner of curses come upon us (Deuteronomy 28). Then, if this goes on long enough, we get cast into the fire and get burned.

We Cannot Win If We Do Not Play "By the Rules"

We must realize that "doing something illegal" means **doing anything against "Yahweh's Word"**. *Yahweh's Word is our "Rule Book"* when it comes to **what to do** but also *how to do it.*

So, if we set out to preach and teach, **but we strive, get angry at people and become offended and accusatory, we resemble more a "work of the flesh" than the fruit of the Spirit**. If we then insult a brother who opposes our doctrine or teaching, we just "broke the commandments" by going against many Scriptures. That's like scoring that touchdown but grabbing a face mask or using "unnecessary roughness" in the process.

Do you see? We must do what Yahweh calls us to do in His Word. **But we must also "follow the Rules" if our "touchdowns" are going to be legal and lasting.** If not, our "works of the flesh" accomplish nothing, will not last and will be burned up. Worse of all, we will incur the very penalties set forth in Yahweh's Word.

This is why the enemy would want to affect our conduct and overall walk with Yahweh: to make us "foul out of the game"; to make us incur penalties and *do "illegal things" that then Yahweh cannot bless nor "back us up" for*. If a football player scores but plays in an "unsportsmanlike manner", the coach will have no choice but to bench him. Also, the coach will not want to sanction or support that player's acts or decisions.

Likewise, if we behave in ways that go against our heavenly Coach, He will not "back us up". He said in His Word that **if we do not forgive others, He will not forgive us**. And, if we're not forgiven, we remain in our sins. And if so, we are not "in right standing with Him". He forgives us **only and if** we forgive others and confess our sins; it is not "automatically". **This is one of the greatest stumbling blocks to otherwise wonderful believers, and the enemy knows it and is why the enemy is behind all _unforgiveness_.**

Therefore, the whole point here is that *the enemy desires to, and is far too successful at, coaching and leading us into* thinking, feeling and acting in *ways that bring us out of a "right standing with Yahweh"*, which, in turn, *causes us to disqualify ourselves, per Yahweh's Word, from receiving* His presence, His power, His authority, His anointing, His blessings and His benefits. And, when that happens, **we may have *religion* but we have *no results***; we may have a form of godliness but **no real power from Yahweh in us, with us or through us**.

Realize It Is the Enemy Working to Affect Our Walk: To Ruin Our Effectiveness

Now, why do I say **it is the enemy** that is affecting us in order to affect our walk before and with Yahweh? Because we have already seen in Chapters 1 and 2 that our battle is against those who can **dwell in our flesh** and **do that which we do not want to do**.

> **Romans 7:17 Now then it is no more I that do it, but sin that dwelleth in me.**
> **18 For I know that in me (that is, in my flesh,) dwelleth no good thing: for to will is present with**

me; but [how] to perform that which is good I find
not.
19 For the good that I would I do not: but the evil
which I would not, that I do.
20 Now if I do that I would not, it is no more I
that do it, but sin that dwelleth in me.

Now remember: we are not "blaming the enemy" to
escape our responsibility. All we are doing is
disclaiming the authorship of evil. We do not
author our evil thoughts, words or deeds anymore
than we author our holy thoughts, words or
deeds. As we said earlier, if all our holy-ness comes
from the Holy One, Who is a Spirit, then why would
our un-holy-ness also not come from a spirit or
spirits of the un-holy kind?

If I cannot "take credit" for the holiness in me,
because I know that I am only yielding, cooperating
and being one with Yahweh in me...why would it not
follow that if I think, feel, talk and act in an unholy
manner, then it is because I am, knowingly or not,
also yielding, cooperating and being one with an
evil spirit of some sort?

Man is always in the middle, making that
decision, and either being led by thoughts, feelings
and words from Yahweh, or, from the enemy (and his
evil, INVISIBLE teachers and helpers), just like in,
and since, the Garden of Eden.

Before Yeshua, no one went around casting out
devils and evil spirits of infirmity and the like out of
people. There are many instances recorded in
Scripture of Yeshua healing physically but also dealing
with "things" that could not be seen: evil spirits. That
is why He came: to destroy the works of the devil.

1 John 3:8 He that committeth sin is of the devil; for the devil sinneth from the beginning. For this purpose the Son of God was manifested, that he might destroy the works of the devil.

That is why when Yeshua came, Scripture says that a great light shone on those that sat in darkness and is also the kind of sight that Yeshua came to restore to the *spiritually* blind as well as the physically blind: because He showed us what we were dealing with that could not previously be seen. He helped **us "see" and discern what really afflicts man**: not a "what", but a "**whom**", and many of them, according to Ephesians 6:12 and the examples of Yeshua.

Isaiah 9:1 Nevertheless the dimness [shall] not [be] such as [was] in her vexation, when at the first he lightly afflicted the land of Zebulun and the land of Naphtali, and afterward did more grievously afflict [her by] the way of the sea, beyond Jordan, in Galilee of the nations.
2 The people that walked in darkness have seen a great light: they that dwell in the land of the shadow of death, upon them hath the light shined.

Matthew 4:13 And leaving Nazareth, he came and dwelt in Capernaum, which is upon the sea coast, in the borders of Zabulon and Nephthalim:
14 That it might be fulfilled which was spoken by Esaias the prophet, saying,
15 The land of Zabulon, and the land of Nephthalim, [by] the way of the sea, beyond Jordan, Galilee of the Gentiles;
16 The people which sat in darkness saw great light; and to them which sat in the region and shadow of death light is sprung up.

Luke 4:18 The Spirit of the Lord [is] upon me, because he hath anointed me to preach the gospel to the poor; he hath sent me to heal the brokenhearted, to preach deliverance to the captives, and recovering of sight to the blind, to set at liberty them that are bruised,

Therefore, we declare again, and I trust that it is clear to you by now, that it is indeed the enemy and his army of evil spirits that greatly affect how so many, and perhaps, most believers, think, feel, talk and act today **and may not even realize it**. Or, **if they do realize, they think it is "themselves" and that the problem is "their sinful nature"**.

It is precisely this that is largely causing "the problem" posed to the reader in the introduction to this book. We are not "recognizing the enemy" enough **because we are not discerning nor differentiating him from ourselves!** The enemy's **evil spirits may well be _in and through_ us but they _are not_ us!** We may have become one with them...**but we are still "us"** and **_they_ are still "them"**. And **_they_** are **_not just thoughts and emotions_**; they are **evil spirits _with_ evil thoughts and evil emotions**. Remember: thoughts and emotions do not exist without a living being.

This is why it is crucial that we stop trying to "control" these thoughts and emotions as if they were "ours" and start casting the evil spirits out instead. When we do, **they go..._and so do their thoughts and emotions_!** Only then do we have any real victory over these "thoughts and emotions".

We must be clear on what we have already Scripturally identified and defined as "sin": **_in_** *addition to* the acts against, or short of, Yahweh's standard, they are **the beings that act, teach and coach us against Yahweh's Word and are present, evil, intelligent beings** that are **unseen** and **dwell in our flesh, in what is the Temple of the Holy Spirit, mostly undetected and unidentified as entities separate from us, that will to do what we do not will to do** (Ephesians 6:12, Romans 7:17-20, 1 Corinthians 3:16-17 and 6:19-20).

Having seen this, we are now ready to see in greater detail just how much the enemy's army is afflicting so many believers to the point that they are not living life more abundantly but rather are having much in their lives being stolen, killed and destroyed (John 10:10). Not only does that **keep them from** being a healthy part of Yahweh's victorious army, but it also leaves them in an emotional and mental "mess".

Worse yet, it can then lead them **to be channels through which the enemy works against other believers** and be **"part of the problem", rather than part of Yahweh's solution**, as we have seen in this and in previous chapters.

"Sin" in Our Temple Afflicts Our Emotional and Mental State

As stated earlier, in this book we do not refer to sin as *"just* the sinful acts" that fall short of Yahweh's standard or Word or that are in disobedience to Him and His Word. **Sin that dwells in the flesh** and **does the sin that we do not want to do is what we war against. We do not wrestle** flesh and blood; **therefore we do not wrestle someone else's flesh or**

our own flesh. We wrestle against those <u>principalities, powers, rulers of the darkness of this world and the spiritual wickedness</u>. In other words, we wrestle against **evil spirits**. Now, let us look closer at **what happens to us, and in us, if and when we have evil spirits dwelling in our flesh**.

In Chapter 5, we considered the question: "who is living in our temple?" According to Scripture, it should **only** be the Holy Spirit of Yahweh living in the temple of Yahweh, which we are:

> **1 Corinthians 3:16 Know ye not that ye are the temple of God, and [that] the Spirit of God dwelleth in you?**

In that chapter, we established that **if** the Holy Spirit is the **only** Spirit living in us and through us, then we ought to manifest **only** the fruit of that Spirit, according to Galatians 5:22-23:

> **Galatians 5:22 But the fruit of the Spirit is love, joy, peace, longsuffering, gentleness, goodness, faith,**
> **23 Meekness, temperance: against such there is no law.**

And what would we be like if we had other spirits, "evil dwellers", <u>working in or through</u> us? Would we even <u>notice</u> such "dwellers" or "helpers"?

The Gadarene Demoniac: Example of a Tormented Person

In Chapter 3, we looked at the man from Gadara who was indwelt by the legion of evil spirits. We examined the effects of those tormenting spirits upon him and listed them from the Scriptural accounts in Mark 5:1 and Luke 8:26. We then saw the fantastic change in the man after Yeshua cast the spirits out of him: he was "sitting at the feet of Yeshua, clothed, and in his right mind".

Let us notice: the spirits that had previously caused the man to be insane and harm and cut himself, once entered into the pigs, drove the pigs insane, driving them into the sea, where they drowned. Pigs normally do not jump off a cliff into the sea but when the devils entered into them, this is exactly what they did.

Therefore, can we conclude that if some of us, or someone we know, is not exactly in his or her "right mind", that it might be due to an evil spirit or spirits? I would submit the answer is "yes". After all, it is certainly not the mind of Christ.

Another Scripture that is revealing but we may be overlooking is 2 Timothy 1:7.

> **2 Timothy 1:7 For God hath not given us the spirit of fear; but of power, and of love, and of a sound mind.**

Something often overlooked in this familiar Scripture is that Paul was encouraging **_Timothy_** about several things such as "let them not despise your youth". In other words, Timothy was being fearful. What we see here is that **Paul was telling him that:**

1. **Yahweh had given him** the Spirit of power, love and a sound mind (**the Holy Spirit**); and

2. Yahweh had not given him the spirit of fear that he was manifesting and being affected by.

Paul was not saying that Timothy did not have the spirit of fear: he was clarifying **that Yahweh had <u>not</u>** given him <u>the spirit of fear</u> <u>that he had</u>. He then adds that the spirit that Yahweh *had* given him was the Holy Spirit.

<u>So who gave Timothy the spirit of fear</u>? Where did it come from? Perhaps from the same source as Adam got his **in Genesis 3 and made him hide from Yahweh.** Remember that?

As soon as he disobeyed Yahweh and ate of the tree of the knowledge of good and evil, he hid because he "was afraid", among his other "negative emotions". Romans 5:12 tells us that through that one man's disobedience, sin entered. That sin <u>that dwells and is</u> <u>"alive"</u> **entered** in.

Well, <u>now Paul tells Timothy that **this fear** he is</u> <u>experiencing does not come from the Spirit that</u> <u>Yahweh has given us</u> (the Holy Spirit) which is of power, love and a sound mind...<u>but from the spirit of</u> <u>fear...which Yahweh has not given</u>. Do you see?

As we saw in Chapters 1 and 2, we now see clearly that "thoughts and feelings" result in actions and that those **thoughts and feelings do not come from "nowhere" or from "thin air"**. Those thoughts and feelings **cannot exist outside or apart from a mind and a living being**. And, **since they do not come from the Holy Spirit**, and since Timothy is either going to have Yahweh's thoughts and feelings <u>or</u> those of another spirit <u>joined to his own</u>, Paul was clarifying to Timothy that ***"fear is not just an emotion" of*** *yours*. It's from the spirit of fear that Yahweh has not given.

From this we see that **even a godly man like Timothy could be affected by an un-holy spirit** that, even in those that behave in socially-acceptable ways, **end up hindering our abundant life and decreasing our effectiveness.**

The Gadarene man suffered from crying and cutting himself, among his bizarre behaviors. We saw in Chapter 3 that modern psychology might classify those as depression and other "conditions". We also saw that the culprit to all his ills was the indwelling of evil spirits in his body, or "sin that dwells in the flesh", **as evidenced by the disappearance of all his ills when Yeshua cast out all the evil spirits**.

So, **could it be** that **some of the "things"** we encounter today in our own lives, which rob us of our joy, peace and enjoyment of life, **might actually be evil spirits that dwell in our flesh**, as Paul candidly admitted that he dealt with? **If fear in Timothy was caused by the spirit** that is not from Yahweh (2 Timothy 1:7), could *worry* and *anxiety* also be caused **by spirits of** *worry* and *anxiety*? *Could anger, bitterness, resentment* and *violence* also be caused by spirits that cause those behaviors? What about *accusation, criticism, sadness, depression, discouragement*, etc? After all, we saw in Chapter 5 that the Holy Spirit would never cause such behavior nor have that fruit. **Could such thoughts and emotions come from the mind of Christ?**

As you have seen by this point, we submit to you (and trust that the Holy Spirit is giving you insight and revelation) that yes, **evil spirits dwelling in the flesh**

of man and **thinking and feeling _through man_** is
what **acts out that fruit and that behavior in man.**

Does This Not Explain Why So Many Believers Think, Feel and Act In Such Un-Holy Ways?

Just tonight, before I sat to write this chapter, I
had the opportunity to encourage and exhort a friend
over the phone. She was wrestling with various
"thoughts and emotions" and, though this person
understands some of the principles taught in this
book, she was so oppressed by those spirits that she
was being driven into thinking, and was arguing back,
that the thoughts and feelings were **caused by** "the
situation" and were, therefore, "inevitable". I countered
with several examples in the Bible where people
displayed **minds, thoughts and emotions that were
contrary to their circumstances** and pointed out to
my friend that circumstances do not, and must not,
necessarily dictate negative, "anti-Word" thoughts and
emotions.

That's when the person who handed me the phone
to encourage my friend said for me to "*pray for peace*"
and "*ask God to give her peace*".

Suddenly, something (*Someone*) rose up inside of
me and said loudly: "***she does not need any more
peace; how much more peace does she need when
the Prince of Peace already lives inside her***!" I
immediately understood what the Spirit of God was
saying to me, which crystallized what I had been
wanting to say to my friend at those moments. So I
said to her: "**the problem is that there are**

tormentors spoiling your peace! <u>**When you get rid of (cast out) the tormenting spirits, the only thing left will be peace!**</u>"

You see, my fellow believer, **peace** can **also** be defined this way: **the absence of torment, agitation or disturbances**. There are all manner of <u>spirits of fear, anxiety, worry, regret, guilt, condemnation</u>, etc. **whose result** <u>is the spoiling of the peace</u>. They torment a person. **In such torment, there can be no peace**.

I pointed out to my friend that it was like having a bunch of people that do not belong in the Temple of God screaming reasons why everything was wrong, bad, worrisome and spoiled. **When ugly things are being screamed, there is no silence and no peace.**

She finally understood that, **as the anointing of the Lord pierced and cut through the madness and the "other voices" agitating her.**

My friend finally understood what I was getting at when I pointed at what Yeshua had done when He cleansed the Temple. <u>When we remove all the "people" that do not belong</u> in the Temple of the Holy Spirit, **then His peace and His fruit will be all that remain** in His temple.

Likewise, **we do not need "more peace", for the Prince of Peace already dwells in us. All we need do is to remove all the spirits that are angry, bitter, critical, accusatory of ourselves and others, and those that are fearful, anxious, hateful and full of torment**, etc., <u>and all that will remain in us will be the One Spirit that is given of Yahweh and is only loving,</u>

joyful, peaceful, faithful, patient, meek, has self-control, etc.

We must only have "one mind". His mind.

Double Minded Believers Are Ineffective Believers

Is this how believers ought to think and feel? Should our thoughts and emotions be dictated by our circumstances? What *should* determine our thoughts and emotions?

The answer is actually more about **Whom** should be determining our thoughts and feelings. According to Scripture, we have the mind of Christ and the Spirit of Yahweh dwelling inside us. Scripture tells us (nay, **commands** us) to be **anxious for nothing** (Philippians 4:6), **fear only He** Who has power to kill the body and then cast into hell (Matthew 10:28) and **take no thought for tomorrow** (Matthew 6:34). We are cautioned to be **angry** (at evil only and **not at flesh and blood**) **and sin not**, forgive always and to **beware lest any root of bitterness spring up and thereby many be defiled** (Hebrews 12:15).

We are called to be loving, patient, kind, meek, humble and seek one another's gain and not our own. **We know** that we are called to these and not to do opposite things like revile evil for evil or railing for railing (1 Peter 3:9). Yet we do it far too often. Why?

I submit to you that we are frequently "double-minded" **because we are having difficulty discerning the spirits** that take us in other directions with the wrong, anti-Scriptural thoughts, feelings, beliefs, actions and ways of thinking.

I submit to you that:

- The fruit of the Spirit and godly behavior is led and caused by the Spirit of God that dwells in us (Galatians 5:22-23, 1 Corinthians 3:16; 6:19) and the mind of Christ, while;
- The "**works of the flesh**" are led and caused by the "**workers**" and "**dwellers**" that may work and dwell in the flesh, that do that which we would not do (Romans 7:17-20), and;
- **We** are to **choose** to **go along with**, and **be led by**, either *the Spirit of God,* <u>OR,</u> *those dwellers* that should not be dwelling nor reigning in our mortal bodies, but <u>from whom we can be delivered</u> thanks to the Lord Yeshua HaMashiach (Romans 6:12, 7:25; Luke 10:17).

While many believers have been taught to deny that they can be affected or even influenced by evil spirits once we are born again, **the following Scriptures clearly refer to believers** that are saved by faith <u>but are continuing to be taught and continue being cleansed, sanctified and made holy by the putting off of sin</u>:

2 Corinthians 7:1 Having therefore these promises, dearly beloved, let us cleanse ourselves from all <u>filthiness</u> of the flesh <u>and spirit</u>, perfecting holiness in the fear of God.

1 Thessalonians 5:23 And the very God of peace sanctify you wholly; and [I pray God] your whole <u>spirit</u> and soul and body be preserved blameless unto the coming of our Lord Jesus Christ.

2 Timothy 2:24 And the servant of the Lord must not strive; but be gentle unto all [men], apt to teach, patient,
25 In meekness <u>instructing those that</u> <u>oppose themselves</u>; if God peradventure will give them <u>repentance</u> to the <u>acknowledging of the truth</u>;
26 And [that] they may <u>recover</u> themselves <u>out of the snare of the devil</u>, who are taken captive by him at his will.

Far too many believers have the same mental and emotional problems that the unbelievers display. Not only do we not display the attributes of God in a consistent manner, we also often seem worse, for sometimes we display and claim attributes of God and at other times we display the attributes of the enemy and the "works of the flesh". <u>As such, the world often sees us as "hypocrites" and the enemy, the accuser of the brethren, has plenty to accuse us of before the rest of the world.</u>

<u>**These things, brethren, ought not so to be**</u>.

James 3:10 Out of the same mouth proceedeth blessing and cursing. My brethren, these things ought not so to be.
11 Doth a fountain send forth at the same place sweet [water] and bitter?
12 Can the fig tree, my brethren, bear olive berries? either a vine, figs? so [can] no fountain both yield salt water and fresh.
14 But if ye have bitter envying and strife in your hearts, glory not, and lie not against the truth.
15 This wisdom descendeth not from above, but [is] earthly, sensual, devilish.
16 For where envying and strife [is], there [is] confusion and every evil work.

Many believers often display just this "duality". It is not to say that we do not sometimes "fail" in our walk. The issue is that many are often influenced and deceived, and therefore think and say, that there are *"reasons why we must agree with, accept and allow"* improper behavior such as that mentioned above. **We must never agree with what is opposite Yahweh's truth and His behavior standards**, which is the same as to "lie against the truth".

I would submit to you that when we behave in such opposite ways, it is because something (or *someone*) is making us "think and feel" in those ways that are opposite the Word of Yahweh. And since the mind of Messiah and the Spirit of Yahweh would never think or feel in such ways, *we must be thinking and feeling the thoughts and feelings of other minds and other spirits seeking to give us those thoughts and feelings...*and they love to hide and let us think that such are "our own"!

It is time that we, as the Body of Christ, understand that those "thoughts and feelings", and the un-Godly beings behind them are not "from us" and begin to repent and renounce our agreement and participation with such beings...and then remove them from our flesh and spirits, as the Scriptures above command.

As stated above, if we do not become single-minded and think and feel only like the One who dwells in us, then we will essentially be double minded. **We must stop being double-minded** for many reasons. First, to stop bringing dishonor to our God (**our "Elohim" in Hebrew**) and stop being "bad ambassadors". Second, to become the people Yahweh has called us to be and "do right" by the price He paid to redeem us and take us unto Himself as His people and possession. Thirdly, and perhaps **most crucial to our walk**, is that <u>we cannot succeed if we are double-minded</u>.

The Danger and Result of a Double Mind: Ineffectiveness

The enemy knows that if he and his army can continue to **stay hidden**, he can continue to **deceive and stumble us**. And his desire, as it always has been, has been to **deceive mankind into acting opposite the Word of Yahweh** and all His commandments, statutes, decrees and ways. And how does he deceive us into acting in such ways? He first gives us thoughts to "convince us" why "it is ok" to go against Yahweh's Word. He gives us <u>reasons that sound correct</u>. He also gives us "feelings" to lead us or downright "push us" in that direction. He is the master of "*therefore*". He shows something that is factual or is there...and then he says "therefore...go ahead and do it". Or, other times he says "therefore...you do not have to do it". Either way, it is **disobedience**, and he deceives us into thinking and feeling it must be or not be that way.

The worst part of his deceiving us into such disobedience is that causing us to fear, doubt or be depressed and discouraged sometimes **is all it takes to make us unstable in all our ways.**

> **James 1:5 If any of you lack wisdom, let him ask of God, that giveth to all [men] liberally, and upbraideth not; and it shall be given him.**
> **6 But let him ask <u>in faith</u>, <u>nothing wavering</u>. For he that wavereth is like a wave of the sea driven with the wind and tossed.**

7 For let not that man think that he shall receive any thing of the Lord.
8 A double minded man [is] unstable in all his ways.

Scripture warns us that we must be in faith and not doubt or waver in our faith or else we will not receive. Such is not the faith that receives from God; we must *diligently* seek Him in order to receive His rewards.

Hebrews 11:6 But without faith [it is] impossible to please [him]: for he that cometh to God must believe that he is, and [that] he is a rewarder of them that diligently seek him.

Seeking Him inconsistently and having faith that wavers **results in us *not receiving*.** We must have steady, unwavering faith and patience to continue in that faith if we are to inherit the promises.

Hebrews 6:11 And we desire that every one of you do shew the same diligence to the full assurance of hope unto the end:
12 That ye be not slothful, but followers of them who through faith and patience inherit the promises.

And so, here's yet **another device of the enemy** that we are not to be ignorant of but often we do not discern. The enemy knows very well that he does not need to eliminate *all* of our faith and walk; **he need only to disrupt the consistency and steadiness of our faith and walk in order to render it largely unsuccessful.** All he has to do is make us fearful and doubtful or unbelieving *sometimes*, or angry, hateful or prideful **some of the time**.

That is often enough to cause us to "miss the mark" of Yahweh's righteous standard in His Word, "disqualify" ourselves from His full blessings <u>and receive curses instead</u>. **All it takes is to withhold forgiveness, or to be bitter against someone, or to worry over finances or other affairs of this life, or to fear or be anxious and "take thought for tomorrow".**

The enemy is **a master at deceiving us into being "out of compliance" with Yahweh's Word**. And he does this by sneaking his invisible army, against whom we wrestle, into our lives and us <u>unwittingly</u> yielding ourselves as the servants to sin, thus becoming joined to them and becoming their servants.

> **Romans 6:16 Know ye not, that to whom ye yield yourselves servants to obey, his servants ye are to whom ye obey; whether of sin unto death, or of obedience unto righteousness?**

Sin in Us Affects Our "Compliance with God"

We have already seen earlier in this chapter how Yeshua taught us to abide in Him and in His Words and have His Words abide in us and to keep His commandments in order to ask and receive and to abide in His love and to bear much fruit. What this essentially teaches us is that ***if we are not keeping His commandments and abiding in His Word, we will ask and not receive.***

We know that we cannot heal people of ourselves but that it is He that heals people through us. We cannot cast out devils of our own; it is He that does it by the finger of God, which is the Holy Spirit. **We cannot do anything without Him**.

Therefore, if He is not with us, "we" cannot heal or set free or cast out the demons out of anyone's lives. We ask and it **shall not be done unto us**. We pray for healing and **no one gets healed**; we pray for someone's situation and **nothing happens**. We pray for marriages and **nothing changes**. We pray for the broken-hearted and **nothing changes**. There is **no power from Yahweh** behind it; **only a form of godliness**. Godliness without any real power or the real God behind it is just another **dead religion**. And that is **not what a life with the only True and Living God is supposed to be like**.

But that is exactly what results if we are not walking with Him in a way that pleases Him. If that happens, He will not be "with us" nor "behind us".

And why would He not be "behind us"? **Scripture is abundant in examples that clearly show that Yahweh does not bless nor fight for nor give victories** to those that either do not do what He has asked or do what He has said not to do. In other words, **He does not bless those that disobey His Word**, which contains all of His commandments. Does He **love them** that disobey? **Yes**. But does He **bless the disobedience? No way**.

If we are going to become victorious in God and with God, we must realize that God's Word does not contain "suggestions that are optional" if we also expect to get blessed. **We certainly have the choice** to comply or not with His Word, but the consequences of that choice are evident since the Garden of Eden and **He has not hidden the consequences to that**

<u>choice</u>: He has made them very plain for us. **If we "comply", we get blessed; if we do not, _not only_ do we not get blessed, but we also get cursed.** In fact, we curse ourselves. We bring the curse upon ourselves.

> **Proverbs 26:2 As the bird by wandering, as the swallow by flying, so the curse causeless shall not come.**

> **Deuteronomy 28:1 And it shall come to pass, <u>if</u> thou <u>shalt hearken diligently unto the voice</u> of the LORD thy God, <u>to observe [and] to do all his commandments</u> which I command thee this day, that the LORD thy God will set thee on high above all nations of the earth:**
> **2 And all these blessings shall come on thee, and overtake thee, if thou shalt hearken unto the voice of the LORD thy God.**

> **Deuteronomy 28:15 But it shall come to pass, <u>if</u> <u>thou wilt not hearken</u> unto the voice of the LORD thy God, to observe to do all his commandments and his statutes which I command thee this day; _that all these curses shall come upon thee, and overtake thee:_**

> **Deuteronomy 30:19 I call heaven and earth to record this day against you, [that] I have set before you <u>life and death, blessing and cursing</u>: therefore <u>choose</u> life, that both thou and thy seed may live:**
> **20 That thou mayest love the LORD thy God, [and] that thou mayest <u>obey</u> his voice, and that thou mayest cleave unto him: for he [is] thy life, and the length of thy days: that thou mayest dwell in the land which the LORD sware unto thy fathers, to Abraham, to Isaac, and to Jacob, to give them.**

This is not an "old testament doctrine" that has "passed away": it is a **timeless principle** supported right through to Revelation. **Obedience brings blessing** and **dis-obedience brings cursing:** *adverse effects of all sorts that cancel, negate and are opposite to all which He calls a blessing.*

> **Mark 11:26 But if ye do not forgive, neither will your Father which is in heaven forgive your trespasses.**
>
> **1 Peter 3:7 Likewise, ye husbands, dwell with [them] according to knowledge, giving honour unto the wife, as unto the weaker vessel, and as being heirs together of the grace of life; that your prayers be not hindered.**

It is clear that, even though Yahweh is merciful and has not dealt with us according to our iniquities, there are too many Scriptures that show that **_He does not bless disobedience: He blesses obedience_**. The New Testament is equally full of calls for obedience.

Having Seen the Enemy's Strategy...How Do We Get "Back In Compliance with Yahweh"?

Having seen that it is indeed the enemy's plan for him and his army to afflict us in ways to cause us to behave and relate un-Scripturally with others, which renders us "out of compliance" with Yahweh, **which in turn render us "disqualified" from His blessings and power and authority**...what are we to do?

The recovery from this snare is succinctly stated in 2 Timothy 2:25-26. Once proper teaching comes and God brings us to the acknowledgement of the truth (which we trust has come by the time you are reading to this point, if not much sooner), we are to **repent and recover ourselves from the snare of the devil**:

> **2 Timothy 2:25 In meekness instructing those that oppose themselves; if God peradventure will give them repentance to the acknowledging of the truth;**
> **26 And [that] they may recover themselves out of the snare of the devil, who are taken captive by him at his will.**

And how do we recover out of this snare?

By beginning to apply the principles stated throughout this book and up to this point:

- **recognizing** and **identifying** the enemies that have thought, felt, acted and talked in and through you;
- taking **responsibility** to choose to do what Yahweh commands;
- **repenting** for participating with each enemy;
- Choosing to **renounce** them and all manner of evil;
- And then **removing** and **casting them out** of your temple, which is your body and mind, **in the Name above all names and by the power of the Holy Spirit**.

Once you see and feel the difference it makes to eject these evil spirits from yourself and others, you will realize, as I and many others have, that this is exactly the kind of discernment and power and authority the Scripture talks about that we ought to have and that was given to us.

> **Hebrews 5:14 But strong meat belongeth to them that are of full age, [even] those who by reason of use have their senses exercised to discern both good and evil.**

> **Matthew 9:8 But when the multitudes saw [it], they marvelled, and glorified God, which had given such power unto men.**

> **Matthew 10:1 And when he had called unto [him] his twelve disciples, he gave them power [against] unclean spirits, to cast them out, and to heal all manner of sickness and all manner of disease.**

> **Luke 9:1 Then he called his twelve disciples together, and gave them power and authority over all devils, and to cure diseases.**

> **Luke 10:17 And the seventy returned again with joy, saying, Lord, even the devils are subject unto us through thy name.**

> **Acts 10:38 How God anointed Jesus of Nazareth with the Holy Ghost and with power: who went about doing good, and healing all that were oppressed of the devil; for God was with him.**

> **1 John 3:8 He that committeth sin is of the devil; for the devil sinneth from the beginning. For this purpose the Son of God was manifested, that he might destroy the works of the devil.**

We have now seen **_only some_** of the many examples of how the enemy and his kingdom (Ephesians 6:12), **largely hidden and masquerading as "our sinful nature" and our "own thoughts and**

feelings", have been and are wreaking havoc on our walk with God and the "compliance" with His Word and way of doing things, which is required for us to have Him working with and through us. This also has been wreaking havoc <u>on our own personal lives, ruining our peace</u> and resulting in us being tormented, worried, fearful, anxious and double-minded, all which in turn **render us** woefully **ineffective and defeated**.

Understanding these things leads us to the solution of how to rectify these situations.

Identifying and **removing** these un-Godly spirits from our temples brings us all back to a "right mind"...a single mind...the mind of Christ. When His Spirit is the only spirit giving us thoughts and feelings, total peace is restored...joy is restored...strength is restored...and faith is **unopposed**. That's when we are <u>free and clear to flow only with the Holy Spirit and be able to walk more consistently than ever before.</u>

This is why these insights are so important!

In the next chapter, we will look at another aspect that suffers terribly when we are tormented emotionally and mentally: our **physical health**.

8

THE ENEMY'S EFFECT ON...
OUR PHYSICAL HEALTH

By now, we have defined the presence of the enemy, ***even amongst ourselves***, as much as we may not want to admit or even consider the possibility that he is *hidden* and *acting* amongst and through ourselves. We have also examined the devastation that the enemy and his army bring into our own state of being, our relationships and even our walk with Yahweh.

Now, let us look at the area of our ***physical health***. Can or does the enemy have an effect upon our health? Does he attack it and if so, how exactly and in what ways? Is there a relationship between sickness and disease and the army of darkness? Is there any connection between ***sin*** and sickness? Is sickness and disease from Yahweh? **Does He want** us in sickness and diseases? Does He want us to die? ***Is He trying to kill us***? Is sickness and disease **the will of God?**

Many of us may think that we know the answers to these questions. Do we also declare that we do not know it all and therefore, are "always open to learning more"? If so, then let us look at these questions with a

fresh and truly open mind and let us look at our "Code of Regulations" and our "Ultimate Authority" to see what the Word of God really does tell us about sickness, disease and God's desires for our health.

Foundational Scriptures About Health, Sickness and Disease

As stated before, we must base ourselves on what the Word of Yahweh says and not on anything else. Also, we must be very **careful in "stretching"** what the Word actually says and we should not take too many liberties when we take a Scripture, then say "*therefore*" and after that, we either form or receive "**a conclusion**" based on that Scripture. I say this because most people say that they base themselves on the Word of Yahweh, yet often have widely differing conclusions. I do not believe we do this "on purpose": we simply "see what we see" and we believe that certain Scriptures take precedence over others. But all the while, our enemy, the deceiver, is the one who is truly "twisting" or "stretching" things **to suggest a "*therefore*"**.

This is why it is very important for us, in this and every other topic, to try to be cautious and keep ourselves "**neutral**" in terms of not being too biased "for or against" any one understanding. If we try to stay truly open to let the Holy Spirit revise our understanding at all times, as He sharpens and adds to our understanding, we can indeed stay on "solid ground" as much as possible.

Having said that, let us look at some Scriptures that speak about sickness, disease and what they all too often, though not always, are connected to.

Is It Yahweh's Will For Us To Have Sickness and Disease?

This first Scripture goes right to this question:

> **3 John 1:2 Beloved, I wish above all things that thou mayest prosper and be in health, even as thy soul prospereth.**

This Scripture tells us that it is of **a high, if not the highest, priority to Yahweh** that we "*be in health*". There is no disputing this statement or this Scripture, for it is plain in the above verse. This Scripture expresses **Yahweh's desire that we be in health**.

This desire of Yahweh's is supported by many other Scriptures in both the Old and the New Testament. And surely, a sick and ailing Body of Believers does not bring as much glory as a healthy Body to the One that says that He is the God who heals you and that He heals our diseases.

> **Exodus 15:26 And said, If thou wilt diligently hearken to the voice of the LORD thy God, and wilt do that which is right in his sight, and wilt give ear to his commandments, and keep all his statutes, I will put none of these diseases upon thee, which I have brought upon the Egyptians: for I [am] the LORD that healeth thee.**

Psalm 103:3 Who forgiveth all thine iniquities; who healeth all thy diseases;

We are **not** condemning, mocking or putting down anyone in sickness and disease presently; **God forbid**. What we are saying is that Yahweh's will for us is to be in health and that ___healing brings more glory to God, more abundant life to us and a better testimony of God___ to a lost and dying world. It shows Him real and true to His Word to an already doubtful world as the One Whose thoughts towards us are of good and not of evil, Who is Mighty above all things and Who has power to heal anything.

We can also glean something else in the above verses: that this health seems to have **a correlation to our soul's prospering**. It seems to be saying that "as your soul prospers, so should, and so does, and/or so will your health prosper". _Judge this in your own heart and see how it seems to you and to the Holy Spirit._

Since we know that our "soul" includes our **mind**, our **emotions** and our **will**, we could also submit to you that, as the mind of Christ is manifested in us, and as we "renew our mind" through the Word of Yahweh, we grow in **thinking, feeling** and **acting _like Him_** more and more. As we come to "think His thoughts" in more and more areas of our lives, we also "agree with Him" and the way He sees everything. Since His Word is Truth (John 17:17), then the more we know and agree with the Truth, the more it shall make us free (John 8:32). And how does it make us free? By using our **will** to choose to agree with, and accept, His Truth and make it also "our Truth", because then it can go ahead to that last step of "making us free".

And, as a man he thinks in his heart, so *is* he (Proverbs 23:7).

Many of us "know the Truth", say, about healing, **but if we also**, at the same time, are full of thoughts and reasons "why I cannot be healed", or why "not everyone gets healed", then the mind-component of the soul may be a "**double mind**". We have already explored the dangers and net effect of having a double mind in the previous chapter. **Therefore, being "single-minded" in our soul can also play a role in having the Truth actually make us free.**

Let us look at two more significant Scriptures:

Acts 10:38 How God anointed Jesus of Nazareth with the Holy Ghost and with power: who went about doing good, and healing all that were oppressed of the devil; for God was with him.

1 John 3:8 He that committeth sin is of the devil; for the devil sinneth from the beginning. For this purpose the Son of God was manifested, that he might destroy the works of the devil.

The first Scripture shows that Yeshua healed and that those healed were being oppressed of the devil. The second Scripture refers to destroying the works of the devil, one of which can be our being *influenced* to sin. And we also see that the Son of God was manifest to destroy the works (plural) of the devil.

Together, these show that when Yeshua healed all that were oppressed of the devil, He was destroying the works of the devil.

We see here an opposite or inverse relationship: the devil does some works, such as being the force or cause behind <u>those that sin and are oppressed</u>, while Yeshua tells us to <u>"sin no more"</u> (John 8:11) and <u>heals all those that were oppressed of the devil.</u>

This **"<u>inverse relationship</u>"** is also expressed clearly in the Scripture we've seen before:

> **John 10:10 The thief cometh not, but for to steal, and to kill, and to destroy: I am come that they might have life, and that they might have [it] more abundantly.**

Therefore, something that is **stealing, killing and destroying in our lives is not from Yahweh** while **everything that resembles life and helps us have it more abundantly,** *this being the reason Yeshua came,* **must be from Yahweh and must be His will.**

<u>Each believer must decide in his or her own heart: does God want me to die of sickness or a disease, or does He want me to be healed and have life, and have it more abundantly</u>?

We know that the enemy comes to steal the Word of God sown in our hearts. He often does it by telling us that "the Word is not true in a particular case **because** ___", and he fills in the blank **with whatever will seem the most "true" to us in our lives**. <u>We must be very careful of this</u>, in regards to every Word and every area of our lives that is addressed by the Word. If we agree with any "reason" that goes against Yahweh's promises, we will not believe. And, if we do not believe it and do not have faith for it, <u>it will be unto us *"according to our faith"*</u>, or lack thereof, and if we do not believe, it will not be possible unto us.

This is one of the enemy's most common, effective and devastating tricks!

One example is to say that Acts 10:38 does not specifically refer only to physical healing, "***therefore***, physical healing is not supported by that Scripture". While that hardly should require a response, it is clear that Yeshua went around healing in every way, shape and form: He healed the **physical body *as well as*** the soul and the broken in heart. We just wanted to make clear that Acts 10:38 **most certainly does include physical healing.** We also recall the Scripture where Yeshua's purpose includes the **full spectrum of healing**:

> **Luke 4:18 The Spirit of the Lord [is] upon me, because he hath anointed me to preach the gospel to the poor; he hath sent me to heal the brokenhearted, to preach deliverance to the captives, and recovering of sight to the blind, to set at liberty them that are bruised,**

This is just more Scriptural support that He came to heal and bring good and not evil.

Just because God is Almighty and there is much evil in our lives, it does not mean that God *desires* for it to be so or to *remain* so.

If someone has us believing that, in this particular situation, "*God is teaching me something*" or "*refining me*", that keeps us from accepting that **God prefers for us to be "healed and made whole" at some point, rather than remain unhealed forever.**

Is There a Connection Between the Presence of Evil Spirits and Physical Sickness and Disease?

Many say "you can't blame evil spirits for everything or for every sickness and disease!" That is certainly true. <u>Let us be perfectly clear about that. We do not.</u>

But, having said that, we ask the reverse: should we blame evil spirits *for <u>no-</u>thing* or *for <u>no</u> sickness and disease*?"

Rather than answer that now, let us simply look and see if there are any Scriptures about that question. Let us see if Yeshua ever dealt with any evil spirits as being connected with any sickness and disease.

> **Luke 13:11 And, behold, there was a woman which had a spirit of infirmity eighteen years, and was bowed together, and could in no wise lift up [herself].**
> **12 And when Jesus saw her, he called [her to him], and said unto her, Woman, thou art loosed from thine infirmity.**
> **13 And he laid [his] hands on her: and immediately she was made straight, and glorified God.**

The above passage speaks for itself: a bowed spine was directly linked to *a spirit of* infirmity.

Let us look at another example:

Matthew 12:22 Then was brought unto him one possessed with a devil, blind, and dumb: and he healed him, insomuch that the blind and dumb both spake and saw.

The above Scripture also clearly shows that blindness and being mute ("dumb") can be caused by a **"corresponding spirit"**.

Another example:

Mark 9:17 And one of the multitude answered and said, Master, I have brought unto thee my son, which hath a dumb spirit;
18 And wheresoever he taketh him, he teareth him: and he foameth, and gnasheth with his teeth, and pineth away: and I spake to thy disciples that they should cast him out; and they could not.
25 When Jesus saw that the people came running together, he rebuked the foul spirit, saying unto him, [Thou] dumb and deaf spirit, I charge thee, come out of him, and enter no more into him.
26 And [the spirit] cried, and rent him sore, and came out of him: and he was as one dead; insomuch that many said, He is dead.
27 But Jesus took him by the hand, and lifted him up; and he arose.
28 And when he was come into the house, his disciples asked him privately, Why could not we cast him out?
29 And he said unto them, <u>This kind can come forth by nothing, but by prayer and fasting</u>.

The above passage is another example of a mute ("dumb") person being so by reason of being "oppressed of the devil". The parallel account in Matthew 17:18 shows that the child was healed and cured once the spirit was cast out:

> **Matthew 17:18 And Jesus rebuked the devil; and he departed out of him: and the child was cured from that very hour.**

But we also see another important point in these Scriptures, which has been used by the enemy to deceive many into unbelief. <u>Notice that the disciples were not able to cast this one out, and therefore, could also not heal the boy.</u> The reason was shown to us by our Master and Teacher: that *this particular kind* does not go out but by **prayer and fasting**.

Many today are often "too quick" to accept <u>and agree with the thought that</u> "not everyone can get healed". As we saw in the example above, the same could have been said, and probably was thought by some in the case of this boy, and yet there was a simple explanation, which the Master gave. Notice that He also said "because of your unbelief". We therefore see that "giving up" and perhaps "not fasting and praying enough" can both be said to be forms of unbelief. Ouch! (Author includes himself.)

Do you see?

If an enemy can whisper, <u>in a thought</u>, that *"this one is too tough"* or *"this is one of those times when it doesn't happen"*, **and "we agree"**, then we quit praying and/or fasting. **And, the moment we** think, or **let ourselves accept, those thoughts and say** *"yeah, I guess this is one of those times when healing doesn't happen"* or *"that spirit does not come out"*, **it will now** ***"be unto us according to our faith", or lack thereof.*** **That is how the enemy tricks us...way more than we might care to admit!**

That is why the solution is to "believe". If it doesn't happen, let it be due to something we do not know or something missing...**but let it not be/may it not be because of our own unbelief, as when Yeshua rebuked the disciples** in the above two accounts.

Here's another example of the connection between evil spirits and infirmities:

> **Luke 8:2 And certain women, which had been healed of evil spirits and infirmities, Mary called Magdalene, out of whom went seven devils,**
> **3 And Joanna the wife of Chuza Herod's steward, and Susanna, and many others, which ministered unto him of their substance.**

This passage is also clear on that connection and nothing more needs to be said.

Last, let us look at Peter's mother-in-law:

> **Luke 4:38 And he arose out of the synagogue, and entered into Simon's house. And Simon's wife's mother was taken with a great fever; and they besought him for her.**
> **39 And he stood over her, and rebuked the fever; and it left her: and immediately she arose and ministered unto them.**

This familiar account shows that the Master actually **rebuked *the fever*.** Each person must decide: did He not rebuke evil spirits? Did He not rebuke the disciples, the Pharisees or other people? Does it not seem clear enough that **one does not rebuke "dead things" or inanimate objects?** *Seek the Holy Spirit and be personally persuaded by Him.* For now, we submit that He did rebuke *a spirit* that caused the fever.

In all fairness, Scripture shows Paul being used to heal someone of a fever and no mention is made of rebuking or of any spirit and he simply laid hands.

> **Acts 28:8 And it came to pass, that the father of Publius lay sick of a fever and of a bloody flux: to whom Paul entered in, and prayed, and laid his hands on him, and healed him**.

The point is that Scriptures do not "cancel each other out" nor does "one cancel the other". **They are meant to be taken _together_, something I personally call "the 'AND' principle". Not "this OR that" but rather, "this AND that".**

As we said earlier, we do not suggest that evil spirits are behind **every** instance of sickness or disease. We simply state that **we must not say "never" just because it is not "always"**. We must **admit if and whenever** it is so. "Sometimes" is neither "always" nor "never".

We must "neither exaggerate nor minimize". But the percentage of these instances may be higher than we thought.

What About Mental or Emotional Sickness and Disease?

Having looked at physical healings that result from dealing with evil spirits, now let us be reminded of the example already mentioned back in Chapters 2 and 3 in the accounts of the Gadarene demoniac in Luke 8 and Mark 5. **His sickness was not physical as much as it was _mental_ and _emotional_ sickness and _disease_.**

That man was greatly tormented by many **evil spirits** and **their** fruit upon him was **certainly not the fruit of the Holy Spirit**: **instead of** love, joy, faith, goodness, meekness, kindness, gentleness, etc, **he displayed a whole other set of emotions and characteristics: rage, crying, violence, isolationism and mental torment.**

As stated before, Yeshua did not seek to solve the outward signs and emotions of **spirits** with **physical or chemical "remedies"**. He **discerned** what was **at the root of** the **behavior**, dealt with "them" directly and simply removed the evil trespassers! And that yielded **the absolute best results: a complete removal of the evil spirits, along with all the fruit of the evil spirits!**

Now, does that not sound like what Yahweh wants for us all: the absolute and total removal of the oppression? I certainly believe so! (I praise Yahweh for having done that very thing in my own life.)

Let us realize this: in order for that to happen, it was necessary to **discern, understand, and recognize the true source and root of the symptoms and then, the key step was to** *remove* **the source...and only then was the best and true "cure" obtained**.

The other case we should recall in this section is the situation with Timothy. Although certainly not as severe as the previous example, Timothy's situation was also the result of a spiritual influence that did not bring peace, but rather, fear. There **is** such a thing as "the spirit of fear" and Paul told this directly to Timothy. We do not know how severe this fear was upon Timothy but it was present enough for Paul to tell him in his letters not to fear or let anyone "despise his youth" and to tell him that the spirit of fear (that he was obviously being influenced by) was not from Yahweh. Whether we realize it or not, Paul tied "the emotions" Timothy was feeling with "the spirit of" those emotions. We all thought that emotions are "just emotions". But now we know better.

Now, before we close this section, I want to point out that in the last two sections of this chapter and in the next two chapters, we will see in greater detail, and more clearly, that a terrible effect of the enemy and his army upon us is to cause us all kinds of "negative emotions", instead of those caused by the Holy Spirit, and that **those negative emotions have terrible ramifications for our physical bodies and our health**. We have already seen in Chapters 6 and 7 how these "negative emotions" are caused by corresponding, tormenting spirits and how that ruins our "mental or emotional health".

Soon, we will see very clearly **just how physically mortal these "negative emotions", which are actually spiritual attacks, can be**.

Please **stay open and keep reading**...for these insights are very powerful and **frequently result in a breakthrough in deliverance, healing or both**. Your miracle could depend on just "one piece" of knowledge or understanding from His Word.

So, How Can We Tell If We Have One of These Cases?

We have now seen but a few of the instances in Scripture where there is a direct link between the presence and oppression of evil spirits and the presence of sickness and disease. Therefore, it is now clear that it is no longer a question of "blaming everything or every sickness and disease on evil spirits". The question now becomes simply a matter of **_"how can we tell if and when we have such cases?_**

The short answer is that we have to have the discernment from the Ruach HaKodesh to tell.

Scripture tells us that part of what Yeshua did was the "recovering of sight to the blind". We have seen and know that Yeshua healed the **physically blind**. But did He not also demonstrate that there was "_more than meets the eye_" in our physical lives? He demonstrated that quite often there were **_spiritual_** **culprits, causes and roots to all sorts of _physical_ ailments, defects and malfunctions.**

Up until Yeshua's ministry on the earth, the evil spirits behind so many physical and emotional conditions _remained largely hidden_. Most people dealt only with the physical results of those that were in reality being "oppressed of the (invisible) devil". And the measures taken were largely physical as well.

But when Yeshua came on the scene, **He demonstrated that there were evil spirits behind all sorts of situations**, and He rebuked them and cast them out, thus remedying the situation "at the root". Whether it was lunatic, bizarre behavior (Matthew 4:24, 17:15, Luke 8:26), curved spines (Luke 13), fevers (Luke 4:39) or even winds and seas (Luke 8:24, Matthew 8:26), **_Yeshua rebuked and cast out and the situations were dealt with in the most effective way!_**

I rather like the account in Luke 8:24, 25, in which we can see something very interesting:

> **Luke 8:24 And they came to him, and awoke him, saying, Master, master, we perish. Then he arose, and rebuked the wind <u>and the raging of</u> the water: and they ceased, and there was a calm.**
> **25 And he said unto them, Where is your faith? And they being afraid wondered, saying one to another, What manner of man is this! for he commandeth even the winds and water, and they obey him.**

Note that in verse 24, He did not just rebuke the water itself: it says He rebuked **the raging of** the water. Did you catch that? He rebuked **the raging** of the elements! Perhaps this shows us that it is <u>not always the physical elements themselves</u>: it was what (*or who*) was stirring up the elements!

These are "points to ponder" with the Holy Spirit.

And so, based on just these few passages of Scripture, we have to admit that Yeshua certainly demonstrated that **quite often, evil spirits cause all sorts of havoc in our physical health**. He also demonstrated how to deal with such. He cast these out by the Holy Spirit and also demonstrated that the Kingdom of God had come unto us and that it was "just part of walking in the Kingdom of God". **We must also do as He did**, and depend on that same Spirit, that dwells in us, to do the works He said we would do and also demonstrate the Kingdom as He did. We must also do it **in the same way He did it: by His Spirit**.

> **Matthew 12:28 But if I cast out devils by the Spirit of God, then the kingdom of God is come unto you.**

Is There a Connection Between the Presence of SIN and Physical Sickness and Disease?

Now that we have seen that **the presence of evil spirits can so often be the direct root and cause of physical illnesses**, let us look at **another, perhaps "less direct" way** in which the enemy and his army can work to have us end up with sickness and disease. Can *sin in our lives* be reason or cause for sickness and disease to come upon us?

Again, let us see what Scripture shows about this:

> **John 5:5 And a certain man was there, which had an infirmity thirty and eight years.**
> **6 When Jesus saw him lie, and knew that he had been now a long time [in that case], he saith unto him, Wilt thou be made whole?**
> **7 The impotent man answered him, Sir, I have no man, when the water is troubled, to put me into the pool: but while I am coming, another steppeth down before me.**
> **8 Jesus saith unto him, Rise, take up thy bed, and walk.**
> **9 And immediately the man was made whole, and took up his bed, and walked: and on the same day was the sabbath.**
> **14 Afterward Jesus findeth him in the temple, and said unto him, Behold, thou art made whole: sin no more, lest a worse thing come unto thee.**

From the above passage, it simply cannot be denied that Yeshua Himself told the man to "**sin *no more***" or else something worse might come upon him. This clearly infers that what had come upon him before had been due to sin. Even if we do not agree with the previous statement, we have to agree that Yeshua is clearly warning that something worse than before, which was a **physical** infirmity, illness or malfunction, could or would come upon him if he were to sin more.

This Scripture alone is enough to pose the principle of connecting sin to an infirmity.

Nevertheless, there is more in Scripture to connect sin with sickness and diseases.

> **Matthew 9:2 And, behold, they brought to him a man sick of the palsy, lying on a bed: and Jesus seeing their faith said unto the sick of the palsy; Son, be of good cheer; thy sins be forgiven thee.**
> **3 And, behold, certain of the scribes said within themselves, This [man] blasphemeth.**
> **4 And Jesus knowing their thoughts said, Wherefore think ye evil in your hearts?**
> **5 For whether is easier, to say, [Thy] sins be forgiven thee; or to say, Arise, and walk?**
> **6 But that ye may know that the Son of man hath power on earth to forgive sins, (then saith he to the sick of the palsy,) Arise, take up thy bed, and go unto thine house.**

The above passage is included in this study to suggest that Yeshua first dealt with the man's sins prior to ministering the physical healing. This point is usually not noted or emphasized in this familiar passage because what is usually emphasized is the demonstration of Yeshua's power to forgive sins on earth, instead of Yahweh only (Mark 2:7, Luke 5:21). That is true; however, Yeshua's **dealing with the sins first** in this instance cannot be denied either.

Again, to be fair, many at this point bring up the *instance* of the man who was blind since birth and the disciples asked Yeshua who had sinned, whether the man or the man's parents. (John 9:2) It is true that Yeshua replied that no one had, but that the particular instance was so that the works of Yahweh would be made manifest in him. The right things to glean and admit from this *instance* is that, while Yeshua did say that no one had sinned, and that there was a purpose for this man's illness, the passage does show the disciples' understanding of the principle of sins' being tied to illness, a principle that is in the Torah and the Scriptures of these Hebrew disciples (this was also borne out in Chapter 7). Secondly, Yeshua did not deny the principle as "wrong in *every* case", as some scholars suggest; He only responded about *this case*. (Remember the principle of "neither exaggerate nor minimize", "the 'and' principle"?)

Lastly, we stated earlier that Yahweh may prefer for us to be healed. Sure enough, the blindness in this passage was there for the sole purpose of showing Yahweh to be the Healer and the "works of Yahweh" to be made manifest!

Now, back to the connection **often** found between sins and sickness and disease.

Could it be that the **sins** were the "**open door**" for this man's palsy? **Could it be** that it is not a Scriptural principle to bless and heal while **sins** are "**left in place**" or "**undealt with**"? Would the **sins** then have been "*a barrier to the blessing*"?

Have we not seen that **Yahweh would not bless Israel with victory while the sin of Achan was in the camp and undealt with**?

> Joshua 7:10 And the LORD said unto Joshua, Get thee up; wherefore liest thou thus upon thy face?
> 11 <u>Israel hath sinned</u>, and they have also <u>transgressed my covenant</u> which I commanded them: for they have even taken of the accursed thing, and have also stolen, and dissembled also, and they have put [it] even among their own stuff.
> 12 <u>Therefore</u> <u>the children of Israel could not stand before their enemies</u>, [but] turned [their] backs before their enemies, because they were accursed: <u>neither will I be with you any more, except ye destroy the accursed from among you.</u>
> 13 Up, sanctify the people, and say, Sanctify yourselves against to morrow: for thus saith the LORD God of Israel, [There is] an accursed thing in the midst of thee, O Israel: <u>thou canst not stand before thine enemies, until ye take away the accursed thing from among you.</u>
> 20 And <u>Achan answered Joshua, and said, Indeed I have sinned against the LORD God of Israel, and thus and thus have I done:</u>
> 25 And Joshua said, Why hast thou troubled us? the LORD shall trouble thee this day. And all Israel stoned him with stones, and burned them with fire, after they had stoned them with stones.
> 26 And they raised over him a great heap of stones unto this day. <u>So the LORD turned from the fierceness of his anger.</u> Wherefore the name of that place was called, The valley of Achor, unto this day.

Notice some of the key aspects underlined above (underlining/emphasis mine):

1. Israel sinned and transgressed His covenant;
2. Therefore, they could not stand against their enemies;

3. Yahweh said He would no more be among them, **except and until**...they destroyed the accursed thing from among them!
4. He said it **twice**;
5. Achan admitted his sin;
6. After the accursed things were removed, and Achan suffered his punishment, <u>then, the Lord turned from the fierceness of His anger</u>; and
7. Afterwards, Israel obtained the victory.

Do we see?

As stated earlier, under the New Covenant, because of what Yeshua did for us, we submit that we have been redeemed from **"the curse of the law"**, meaning, **the penalty of death**. And that is a good thing, because, otherwise, we'd have to die like Achan did <u>every time we sin such sins</u>.

But, the principle remains and so do the curses, such as sickness and diseases, as listed in Deuteronomy 28:16-68.

If our enemies are **spiritual** <u>armies of darkness</u>, just like Israel's enemies were **physical** <u>armies</u>, would **the same principles not hold true** with the **same Elohim**, Who **changes not**, and is **the same yesterday, today and forever**?

We just saw it: **we cannot stand against our enemies when we sin and transgress His Covenant.**

So, **could it be that, if we transgress, we cannot stand against our spiritual, invisible enemies,** who then can smite us and defeat us (Joshua 7:4, 5)?

I submit to you that this is true, whether it's the "Old" or the "New" Covenant. His Covenant has had some "upgrades" and was moved into our hearts but essentially remains.

> **Jeremiah 31:33 But this [shall be] the covenant that I will make with the house of Israel; After those days, saith the LORD, I will put <u>my law in their inward parts, and write it in their hearts;</u> and will be their God, and they shall be my people.**

Having shown this principle of "dealing with sins before the victory, the blessing and His presence", we add that the reason we pointed this out is because it also connects with, and sheds light on, another familiar passage of New Covenant Scripture:

> **James 5:14 Is any sick among you? let him call for the elders of the church; and let them pray over him, anointing him with oil in the name of the Lord:**
> **15 And the prayer of faith shall save the sick, and the Lord shall raise him up; and if he has committed sins, they shall be forgiven him.**
> **16 Confess [your] faults one to another, and pray one for another, that ye may be healed. The effectual fervent prayer of a righteous man availeth much.**

In verse 15, let us notice that it says that if the sick person "...has committed any sins, they <u>shall be</u> forgiven him." Many understand this passage to mean that the sins are "also covered and forgiven **automatically**" through this anointing in the name of the Lord and prayer by the elders. I myself also used to think so. But if we connect this to the previous passage, we see that what is being described is that the sins "***must also***" (**shall**) be dealt with, and be forgiven him, as part of receiving the healing. If this was not the case, <u>realize that it would be like authorizing that sins be "left in place"...and still receive healing and blessing</u>!

Realize also that verse 16 says "to confess", as well as pray, for one another, "that ye may be healed". Do you see that? It's saying that, in order to be healed, "confess and pray" is necessary.

Why confess? Because **we must confess our sins if we are to be forgiven**! Is there "***automatic*** forgiveness" in Scripture **without *repentance* and confession**? (Nehemiah 9:1, 2; I John 1:9.)

John the Baptist preached repentance; Yeshua preached repentance and instructed His disciples to preach repentance; Peter instructed men to repent on the day of Pentecost, Yeshua tells five of the seven churches in Revelation to repent, etc.

As before, we submit these points to the reader as shown in Scripture, but as with any truth of the Scripture, whether obvious or not-so-obvious, it must be the Spirit of Yahweh that gives us **revelation** about the **information**.

We leave this up to the reader to consider in his heart and with the Holy Spirit within each born-again Believer.

Is Sickness and Disease a Blessing or a Curse? Can We Receive Blessings Without Obedience? Isn't Disobedience Sin?

The next part of this chapter deals with the above three questions as one set because they are so closely tied together. We also want to point out that they involve **very powerful principles** that have **very important ramifications**. For a great many, these have revealed what was **hidden, hindering** or downright **preventing** a healing for years!

Deuteronomy 28 is often referred to as *"the blessings and the curses"* because it lists the blessings and the curses that Yahweh said could be upon His people. Many in the Body of Believers often quote things such as "being the head and not the tail" and have been taught that, somehow, through Yeshua HaMashiach, we have the **blessings** *automatically* **with no curses** whatsoever.

What we do not often realize is that the **blessings are _conditional_ upon obedience** and **hearkening** unto Yahweh while the **curses are *also* conditional upon disobeying** and **not hearkening** to Yahweh.

It is extremely important to realize that *the blessings do not include "sickness and disease"* of any kind. *However, the curses absolutely do include all manner of sickness and disease*!

For anyone that says that they "have been redeemed from the curse of the law", we have just one question below. But first, we just want to say that this issue can be a whole other study that we do not want to get too deeply into in the scope of this book. For now, suffice it to just remind ourselves that Scripture teaches that the Law and his Word would never pass away until all be fulfilled (which has not yet been) and that we were only redeemed from *the curse of* the law, meaning **the penalty of death** for non-compliance of the whole law! That in no way "cancels out" the rest of the law, which includes Deuteronomy 28 and all of Yahweh's standards in His Word that still stand.

Having said that, **here's the one question** for anyone that disputes that Deuteronomy 28 still stands: **if the curses no longer apply...and we have been redeemed from them,** *then why is there so* *much sickness and disease, as listed in verses* *16-68 of that chapter, present in those Believers* *that have been "redeemed" from those curses?*

The mere presence of any of those curses must mean that "something is missing". Something is "blocking our blessings" and replacing them far too often with curses. What could that be? **Could it be anything like the sin of Achan discussed earlier**?

For now, we will only look at the key passages that show the conditions of the blessings and the curses. We also note that the blessings are listed in verses 3-14 (12 verses) while the curses are listed in verses 16-68 (53 verses).

> **Deuteronomy 28:1 And it shall come to pass, if thou shalt hearken diligently unto the voice of the LORD thy God, to observe [and] to do all his commandments which I command thee this day, that the LORD thy God will set thee on high above all nations of the earth:**

> **2 And all these blessings shall come on thee, and overtake thee, if thou shalt hearken unto the voice of the LORD thy God.**

As you can see, it says twice that these blessings shall only come and overtake us *"if"* we do as they ask: hearken, observe and do.

Now, let's look at the introduction to the curses.

> **Deuteronomy 28:15 But it shall come to pass, if thou wilt not hearken unto the voice of the LORD thy God, to observe to do all his commandments and his statutes which I command thee this day; that all these curses shall come upon thee, and overtake thee:**

Similarly, we see that the curses will also only come and overtake us *"if"* we do as it says, the opposite of the above: **not** hearken to observe and do.

Let me be quick to point out for those that might be reasoning in their hearts: I am not talking about "**having to do** anything *to be saved*". I am **not talking about salvation**. I am **talking about *the blessings*.**

Salvation is indeed not by the works of the law, for by the deeds of the law shall no flesh be justified; we are saved by faith, and not of works, lest any man should boast (Romans 3:20, 28; Ephesians 2:8, 9).

The love of God is unconditional, indeed. **However, His blessings are His rewards** and, although He has certainly "not dealt with us according to our iniquities", by having provided salvation and forgiveness through Messiah, this in no way means that we get rewarded while continuing in any and all disobedience to his Word.

Does the New Covenant not demand "obedience"? Are we allowed to "do whatever we want"? Did not Paul answer *"God forbid"* when he talks about 'shall we continue in sin that grace may abound"?

> **Romans 6:1 What shall we say then? Shall we continue in sin, that grace may abound?**
> **2 God forbid. How shall we, that are dead to sin, live any longer therein?**

We know that these questions are not just "one-dimensional" and that they have to do with our <u>overall understanding</u> of more than just a few verses. Therefore, we leave some of this topic, as stated, as "a whole other study beyond the scope of this book". However, it cannot be denied that any "New Testament Believer" knows that **the New Testament says in many ways that we should not sin**. And sin is "transgression of the law", whether written in stone **or in our hearts now under the New Covenant**.

> **1 John 3:4 Whosoever committeth sin transgresseth also the law: for sin is the transgression of the law.**

This actually gives us <u>the answer to the third of the three questions</u> we posed in this section: disobedience to His law will be a transgression of Yahweh's law, and that is sin. Therefore, we see that "**disobedience is sin**".

We also have seen the <u>answer to the second question</u>: that Yahweh does <u>not</u> give blessings without "hearkening to observe and do" (Deuteronomy 28).

Let us now seal the answer to the first, and perhaps greater, of our original three questions: *is sickness and disease a blessing or a curse?*

The short answer (as we hinted earlier) is that sickness and diseases are simply not listed in verses 3-14 of Deuteronomy 28. You guessed it: **sickness and diseases are listed under verses 16-68. Those are indeed *the curses*.**

Let us look at *just some of the curses and see if we have any of them* among the "redeemed":

> **Deuteronomy 28:21 The LORD shall make the pestilence cleave unto thee, until he have consumed thee from off the land, whither thou goest to possess it.**
>
> **22 The LORD shall smite thee with a consumption, and with a fever, and with an inflammation, and with an extreme burning, and with the sword, and with blasting, and with mildew; and they shall pursue thee until thou perish.**
>
> **27 The LORD will smite thee with the botch of Egypt, and with the emerods, and with the scab, and with the itch, whereof thou canst not be healed.**
>
> **28 The LORD shall smite thee with madness, and blindness, and astonishment of heart:**
>
> **29 And thou shalt grope at noonday, as the blind gropeth in darkness, and thou shalt not prosper in thy ways: and thou shalt be only oppressed and spoiled evermore, and no man shall save [thee].**
>
> **32 Thy sons and thy daughters [shall be] given unto another people, and thine eyes shall look, and fail [with longing] for them all the day long: and [there shall be] no might in thine hand.**

34 So that thou shalt be mad for the sight of thine eyes which thou shalt see.

35 The LORD shall smite thee in the knees, and in the legs, with a sore botch <u>that cannot be healed</u>, from the sole of thy foot unto the top of thy head.

59 Then the LORD will make thy plagues wonderful, and the plagues of thy seed, [even] <u>great plagues, and of long continuance, and sore sicknesses, and of long continuance.</u>

60 Moreover he will bring upon thee <u>all the diseases of Egypt</u>, which thou wast afraid of; and they shall cleave unto thee.

61 <u>Also every sickness, and every plague, which [is] not written in the book of this law,</u> them will the LORD bring upon thee, until thou be destroyed.

65 And among these nations shalt thou find no ease, neither shall the sole of thy foot have rest: but the LORD shall give thee there <u>a trembling heart, and failing of eyes, and sorrow of mind:</u>

66 And thy life shall hang in doubt before thee; and thou shalt <u>fear</u> day and night, and shalt have <u>none assurance of thy life</u>:

67 In the morning thou shalt say, Would God it were even! and at even thou shalt say, Would God it were morning! for the <u>fear of thine heart</u> wherewith thou shalt <u>fear</u>, and for the sight of thine eyes which thou shalt see.

Let's be plain about it: **Scripturally speaking, if we have sickness and disease, we have some of the curses.**

Now, I know that such a statement immediately makes many uncomfortable because the implication is: "*Am I in sin?*" **Let me say: it is not just because of this one reason**. It could certainly be because we do not take care of our bodies properly, or because we defile our body (1 Corinthians 3:17), or because we do not discern the Lord's body (1 Corinthians 11:29, 30). But, it could also certainly be because of the above Scriptures...especially in light of Proverbs 26:2.

> **Proverbs 26:2 As the bird by wandering, as the swallow by flying, so the curse causeless shall not come.**

The Word tells us that curses do not come without a cause or reason.

Therefore, we simply cannot deny that having sins, according to Scripture, certainly "works against us" in trying to obtain healing.

All we can say is: Yahweh's Word promises blessings if we obey and curses if we disobey. It makes Scriptural sense.

This does not mean that we <u>must</u> be in sin **_knowingly._** Could it be that we might be "in sin" **and not even know it?** That is certainly possible.

> **Hosea 4:6 My people are destroyed for lack of knowledge: because thou hast rejected knowledge, I will also reject thee, that thou shalt be no priest to me: seeing thou hast forgotten the law of thy God, I will also forget thy children.**

> **Isaiah 5:13 Therefore my people are gone into captivity, because [they have] no knowledge: and their honourable men [are] famished, and their multitude dried up with thirst.**
> **14 Therefore hell hath enlarged herself, and opened her mouth without measure: and their glory, and their multitude, and their pomp, and he that rejoiceth, shall descend into it.**

Therefore, we see from Scripture that **lack of knowledge can** be the **cause** of **dire consequences**.

Nevertheless, even if that's the case, **there are ways out** of that situation and we also find that in Scripture.

> **James 1:5 If any of you lack wisdom, let him ask of God, that giveth to all [men] liberally, and upbraideth not; and it shall be given him.**
> **6 But let him ask in faith, nothing wavering. For he that wavereth is like a wave of the sea driven with the wind and tossed.**
> **7 For let not that man think that he shall receive any thing of the Lord.**
> **8 A double minded man [is] unstable in all his ways.**

We point out that in order to receive that wisdom, we must ask in faith and not waver, which the Scripture calls being "double minded" and unstable. Recall that the dangers of a double mind were discussed earlier in Chapter 7.

If there's hidden sin in us, we should be eager to ask Yahweh to show us, that we may repent of it and put it away, **for He pardons abundantly** (Isaiah 55:7). This should be of comfort and encouragement to us, so we will not be "unwilling to entertain and explore the possibility". **If we do, the enemy and his army have us right where they want us**!

Now, also recall that we also examined **the trap** we get into if we get "out of compliance with Yahweh" back in Chapter 7. Remember also what we have established in earlier chapters: we do not always do this "on purpose". **The enemy's army is just very**

good in hiding and giving us "thoughts and feelings" designed to "drive us" into doing wrong and opposite whatever verse of Scripture he can make us transgress...*because they know that we are the ones who suffer if we get "out of compliance".*

Could it be as simple as "taking thought for tomorrow"? Or unforgiveness? Or being "sore at somebody"? Could it be as simple as having in us some of the things that it says to put off and put away in Ephesians 4 and Colossians 3?

We leave these questions also for the reader to meditate upon as things to consider. If we are not obeying these, or any other things in Scripture, **we will be transgressing** like it says in 1 John 3:4.

Now, let us look at some specific Scriptures that speak directly about certain sicknesses and diseases. These are Scriptures that Believers often have only heard or read once or twice, or in passing, or not at all.

Medical Realities That Have Scriptural References

We have looked at Scriptures that show us sickness and diseases that are evidently and directly caused by the presence of "corresponding spirits". We have also seen "spirits of infirmity". We have seen evil spirits causing mental and emotional torment as well. And we have just examined the connections between sin and sicknesses, including the "open door" that sin, disobedience and transgression can be to "qualify us" for the curses in Yahweh's Word.

Now, let us look at what is perhaps an even **less direct or less obvious way** in which the enemy and his army can work in us **to cause us to end up with sickness and disease**. *This "route of attack" may also be the most devastating* precisely because it is "less obvious" and **because it has a very wide and far-reaching potential to bring all kinds of imbalances and malfunctions upon our physical bodies**.

Read on!

While improper nutrition, environmental contaminants and other **physical factors** certainly create or contribute to sickness and disease, the medical community has been realizing and reporting for some time now that what many call **"negative emotions"** may be the underlying cause of much sickness and disease. Things like **"stress"**, **fear** and **anxiety** are now being credited with being at the heart of many diseases such as cardiovascular diseases, allergies, cancer, autoimmune diseases and much more. A report estimated some time ago that **up to 80% of all incurable diseases may be linked to "toxic emotions" such as fear, anxiety, stress and others**.

This is also often referred to as the "*mind-body connection*". But we who are spiritual could go further and say "*spirit-soul-body connection*".

This is not a new concept to believers, as it has been around for some time. After all, the Bible does have something to say about this.

Let us look at just a few areas to suggest to the reader some of the many possibilities that are being documented in the last 20 years as **medical realities that have a Scriptural basis**.

A Wounded Spirit

> **Proverbs 17:22 A merry heart doeth good [like] a medicine: but a broken spirit drieth the bones.**

> **Proverbs 18:14 The spirit of a man will sustain his infirmity; but a wounded spirit who can bear?**

The above two verses tell us that being merry of heart is like medicine and that a man's spirit will sustain his infirmity. But they also tell us that a wounded spirit may be tough or impossible to bear and that **a "broken spirit" can dry up the bones!**

Envy

Proverbs 14:30 seems to echo the good effect of a sound heart for the physical body. It also speaks more specifically about how a certain "emotion" may have direct physical consequences.

> **Proverbs 14:30 A sound heart [is] the life of the flesh: but envy the rottenness of the bones.**

The above Scripture is **specifically addressing _envy_** and also its effect on the bones: **rottenness**.

While many could speculate as to what it means when the Word of Yahweh says *"dries up the bones"* and *"rottenness to the bones'*, it would not be difficult for those that have some medical background to come up with some of the effects that would be included by these descriptions from the Word.

Perhaps the first guesses we could have for these descriptions might be things like <u>arthritis</u> and <u>osteoporosis</u>.

Another aspect is that it is known that bone marrow is what is involved in the manufacture of one of the main components of the body's immune system: white blood cells. As many will know, white blood cells are the ones that go around the body destroying things that are identified as "invaders", or otherwise harmful, to the body.

Therefore, it is easy to see how far-reaching it might be if just the bones and the bone marrow can be <u>affected by "things" like envy and a broken spirit</u>. **Many other diseases** have to do with disorders related to the bones, the bone marrow or the health of the immune system that is so dependent on the health of the bones.

Hope Deferred

Another Scripture is:

> **Proverbs 13:12 Hope deferred maketh the heart sick: but [when] the desire cometh, [it is] a tree of life.**

This Scripture brings up the issue that "hope deferred" can affect the heart and "make it sick". Perhaps "hope deferred" is referring to things such as *disappointments, being disillusioned, hopelessness, sadness, grief, sorrow* and the like.

We could also ask ourselves what it means when it says they make the heart sick. **Surely Yahweh knows**.

Could this have anything to do with the variety of **heart disorders**?

Fear

Fear, anxiety and stress disorders, as far as the medical community is concerned, are thought to be underlying all types of cardiovascular diseases such as heart attacks, high blood pressure and the like. The Scriptures that come to mind are the above Scripture and also this one:

> **Luke 21:26 <u>Men's hearts failing them for fear</u>, and for looking after those things which are coming on the earth: for the powers of heaven shall be shaken.**

Let us look at just one example in order to explain how the enemy may be behind all this.

The medical community knows <u>the mechanics, or the "how"</u>, of many diseases. As our example, let us take high blood pressure. **High blood pressure** is the result when the walls of the arteries and veins of the body harden. As they harden, they become less elastic, stiffen and become constricted. As a result, the blood does not flow freely enough and there is an actual "backflow" of blood. The narrowing of the arteries, combined with this "backflow", creates higher pressure and that, in turn, makes the heart have to "work harder". This extra work places extra stress on the heart. And that causes all sorts of problems.

This is a very simplified look at the "how" of this condition. **But *why* does it happen in the first place? What *causes* the stiffening and hardening of the walls of the arteries?** If you said "fear, anxiety and stress", you are in agreement with what the medical community has been starting to admit now for about 20 years or more, depending on who you talk to.

Now, let us talk about what we have been talking about in this book prior to this chapter.

Some would say that "*we cannot help but be in fear*". Many say that "*as long as we are in this body of flesh, we are going to feel fear and we cannot help it*". Others say that "*the state of the world inevitably leads us to fear*".

Does Yahweh agree with these statements? Does He want us to fear? Does He command us to fear? What did Yeshua tell His disciples about fear? Are we supposed to fear?

> **John 14:1 Let not your heart be troubled: ye believe in God, believe also in me.**
>
> **John 14:27 Peace I leave with you, my peace I give unto you: not as the world giveth, give I unto you. Let not your heart be troubled, neither let it be afraid.**
>
> **Luke 21:26 <u>Men's hearts failing them for fear</u>, and for looking after those things which are coming on the earth: for the powers of heaven shall be shaken.**

We could list many other Scriptures, but the short answer is that the Word so very often says to **"fear**

not". We are to fear (in holy awe, respect, reverence and honor) Yahweh only.

Therefore, I have another question. <u>If Yahweh does not want us to fear</u> or live in fear, ***then who does***? <u>Where is fear coming from</u>? <u>What is fear</u>? And if we are <u>gripped</u> by reasons to fear, **that are not Yahweh's "reasons"**, then ***could something or someone else be teaching us to fear***?

Consider the following Scriptures carefully before we make our final point to you.

> **2 Timothy 1:7 For <u>God hath not given</u> us <u>the spirit of fear</u>; but of power, and of love, and of a sound mind.**

> **1 John 4:16 And we have known and believed the love that God hath to us. God is love; and he that dwelleth in love dwelleth in God, and God in him.**

> **1 John 4:18 There is no fear in love; but perfect love casteth out fear: because fear hath torment. He that feareth is not made perfect in love.**

We already saw in Chapter 5 that God **has only given us one spirit, the Holy Spirit**, to dwell in us. We also saw the "emotions" and characteristics of the Holy Spirit are listed in Galatians 5:22-23. **The fruit of the Holy Spirit, given to us by Yahweh, does not include fear.** That is why Paul is telling Timothy that Yahweh has not given him "the spirit of fear" that is giving him fear. We see here that ***there is such a thing as a spirit of fear***.

Fear "is not *just* an emotion". It is an emotion. But **it is *also* a spirit** and **that spirit gives that**

emotion, **just like Yahweh is a Spirit, and He is love, and Yahweh the Spirit gives us and brings us love.**

Therefore, beloved brethren, I submit to you, and pray that the Spirit give you revelation, about these last few statements and the next few statements.

- We have established since the start of this book/study that "thoughts and feelings" come from living spirits, whether good or bad, holy or un-holy.
- These evil spirits against whom we wrestle do not make themselves known, nor announce their presence, and give us "thoughts and feelings" as if those were "our own", in order to lead us into "agreeing" and acting in ways opposite the Word of Yahweh that we know.
- They get us "in sin" and "out of compliance with Yahweh" and also directly torment our lives, **all of which ruin our relationships at home, at work, at the congregation, and with ourselves and with Yahweh.**

Now, **what if they also know that, if they can get us all worked up with fear and anxiety, our bodies will react adversely?** What if they know our biology and chemistry better than us? What if they, as **our enemies, smite us in our emotions and thoughts, which in turn, determine all kinds of effects on our bodies, like high blood pressure?**

This principle also works on all the other systems of the body besides the cardiovascular system!

Medical science has long known that **all kinds of chemical, hormonal and neurotransmitter**

functions are affected by our emotions. Our respiratory, digestive, nervous, musculo-skeletal, endocrine, limbic, sympathetic, parasympathetic and other systems are all affected by our emotions!

Things like the "fight or flight" response are triggered by fear or crises situations. **What happens in our bodies if we feel like we are in such situations constantly?**

Things like **cortisol** and **adrenaline** are secreted as a result of stress. Too much time spent feeling "stress emotions" results in too much cortisol and adrenaline, which affect the body in many detrimental ways **and result in many sicknesses and diseases, like allergies, just to name one that many *believers* have.**

Depression

Even our mental condition is affected by emotions. An example of this is what is known as **depression**.

The "how" of depression can be briefly explained in the following way. **Serotonin**, secreted by the hypothalamus gland, is what makes us "feel good", emotionally speaking. But, if thoughts and feelings of "**depression**" or of other sad or depressing thoughts, like "**not feeling loved**", come at us and we agree with them, dwell on them, then the hypothalamus responds to those "thoughts and feelings" and now secretes less serotonin! **As its levels decrease, we become "depressed".**

Sadly, instead of getting rid of the evil spirits that **lead us to dwell in, think and feel**, those "negative thoughts and feelings", which are essentially **the fruit of un-holy spirits**, most doctors prescribe a "serotonin enhancer", which simply keeps the lower serotonin levels in the blood system longer and make us "feel better" that way. Unfortunately, that just "masks" our true problem, **which is nothing less than us being afflicted by evil spirits**. Plus, this also **gets us dependent on prescription drugs** and adds to us the **side effects** and **financial burden** associated with these "medicines".

Do we see?

Remember when we discussed "seeking to solve spiritual issues with physical or chemical means"?

I, and many others, have come to realize something that the enemy also knows: **all he and his army have to do is "hijack and capture our thoughts and emotions" and then our bodies will inevitably react in many negative ways, resulting in elevated levels of "all the bad stuff" and lowered levels of "all the good stuff"!**

Isn't this absolutely alarming? Isn't there a way out?

There is!

The next chapter gives us a glimpse into "*A More Excellent Way*".

9

A MINISTRY CALLED
"BE IN HEALTH™"

By now, it must be very apparent to the reader that **the enemy and his army have been "hijacking our thoughts and feelings" in many areas** and that this in turn can, and far too often does, have **devastating consequences** on just about every area of our lives.

Worse yet is that all this devastation, upon us, our relationships, our families, our walk with God and even our physical health, **often happens without us being fully aware of what is really happening or why**.

Some blame **only** the devil. Some blame **only** the people. Some even blame **only** God. All this "blaming only one factor" can result in a real attack on our faith if we do not place **the right amounts** of blame *correctly where the right amounts belong*. And that is exactly what happens if we do not properly understand and discern what is really happening. It can cause us to "give up" on our faith and on God if we try and fail over and over and finally succumb to discouragement and defeat. Even worse, we can end up **bitter at people or at God**, <u>neither of which we really wrestle with</u>.

It also results in the present situation we have with many, or most, in the body of Christ. If we do not discern that it is really the enemy cleverly ***causing us to err in many ways in which we actually hurt ourselves***, we continue causing ourselves and our loved ones a world of hurt. We also continue preaching that Yahweh loves, heals and is powerful to act in mighty ways on our behalf **but have very little real results to show it**.

That is exactly what brought a certain pastor at a certain point in his walk to ask God why only 5% of the people he was praying for were getting healed. The Lord answered him and the answers have led to **many wonderful clarifications to the Scriptures that**, in the opinion of many, including myself, **truly enable us to be the Body of Believers that we are supposed to be.**

For the last twenty years, this pastor has dedicated himself to the service of the Body in ministering these Scriptural truths to the people and simply letting the Lord confirm His Word with signs and wonders following, ***resulting in healing and deliverance to thousands, just as His Word promises.***

In short, it could be said that the essence of what the Lord clarified for him was that **the enemy's army was often <u>covertly</u> causing us to sin**, often **unknowingly, and resulting in sickness, diseases, and disobedience that was preventing Him from blessing us.**

Another factor was that there was **often a lack of knowledge** about God's Word **in certain areas.** That lack of knowledge can result in **destruction and captivity**.

> **Hosea 4:6** My people are destroyed for lack of knowledge: because thou hast rejected knowledge, I will also reject thee, that thou shalt be no priest to me: seeing thou hast forgotten the law of thy God, I will also forget thy children.

> **Isaiah 5:13** Therefore my people are gone into captivity, because [they have] no knowledge: and their honourable men [are] famished, and their multitude dried up with thirst.

> **Proverbs 8:33** Hear instruction, and be wise, and refuse it not.

Many do not like to have it suggested that they might be in disobedience or lacking knowledge and not know it. They often react with offense. But God's Word above warns that we should not reject knowledge or more of it. We must be careful to not reject knowledge when suggested. **We should examine the possibility and remain "teachable" and be at least willing to review a matter before rendering judgment**.

I and many others have been delivered, healed and set free by being open to hearing the insights from God's Word that this pastor has to share.

Please allow me to tell you just a little about this pastor and his ministry based in Thomaston, GA: a ministry called *Be In Health*™

Credit and Honor Unto Whom It Is Due

> **Romans 13:7** Render therefore to all their dues: tribute to whom tribute [is due]; custom to whom custom; fear to whom fear; honour to whom honour.

As stated in the *"Acknowledgements"* page, many of the foundational principles discussed in this book are from the insights and teachings credited to Pastor Henry W. Wright and his ministry, *Be In Health™*, based in Thomaston, GA.

As he sought the Lord for answers about the health of his sheep, the Lord clarified some Scriptural truths that held the keys to what was quite often at the root of much sickness and disease.

Today, Pastor Henry and his ministry (which conducts conferences and teachings locally and worldwide) are collectively recognized by both the medical community and the Body of Believers as being on the "cutting edge" of research and insight into the connection between the spirit, soul and physical body. Pastor Henry works **in complete harmony with the medical profession**, and ***not against it***, in gaining understanding about how our "whole being" really functions.

> **1 Thessalonians 5:23 And the very God of peace sanctify you wholly; and [I pray God] your whole spirit and soul and body be preserved blameless unto the coming of our Lord Jesus Christ.**

In more than 20 years of ministry, Pastor Henry's ministry is credited with thousands of documented healings and miracles in many types of conditions and diseases, **many of which are deemed incurable by medical science.**

As Pastor Henry himself declares, it is God Who does all the healing. He only ministers the Word of God and the insights God has given Him from His Word to the Body of Believers. He is truly a pastor according to God's heart.

> **Jeremiah 3:15 And I will give you pastors according to mine heart, which shall feed you with knowledge and understanding.**

I personally thank God often for *Be In Health™*, Pastor Henry and for the awesome benefits to my life and my walk with God since I found out about them in 2005.

How I Found Out About Be In Health™

I found out about *Be In Health™* during the most difficult time of my life, as I was facing the death of my marriage. My wife had found out about *Be In Health™* while searching about healing for one of her sisters. She attended *Be In Health™*'s one-week program in November of 2004 with her two sisters. Soon afterwards, she told me that I also would have to attend before we could be reunited, as we were already separated at the time.

The Lord soon revealed to me that I was indeed to go and instructed me to "go for two weeks", to which I agreed without even knowing what that meant, since I knew nothing of *Be In Health™* or their programs. I attended those two weeks in May 2005.

As I soon found out, *Be In Health™*'s first one-week program is called *"For My Life"* and they also had a second one-week program called *"For Their Life"*. The first program is intended for a person to focus on their **own life** (and even their ancestry) and **examine every area** of it through its **whole lifespan**, even before birth, **in the light of Scripture**. The second program is intended to go further in those insights with an emphasis on helping to minister those same insights to others.

The objective is simple yet powerful: **to evaluate how our lives line up with God's Word** *and then* **to** *choose* **to line up with God and His Word in any and all areas that He reveals are "out of line".**

The result of the above objective, according to Scripture, leads us to receive His blessings and remove any hindrances or blocks to receiving fully from Him. In fact, according to Scripture, **this is what we all are usually trying to achieve, and should be doing anyway** every day of our lives.

While I was not actually sick with any physical sickness or disease in May of 2005, I had just begun to feel like I was going to be soon. Somehow, I <u>knew</u> this was happening to me as a result of my deep despair, grief and hopelessness.

You see, it had become certain to me that my marriage was going to fail. The sense of loss, grief and despair had become too much for me to bear any longer. I truly was at the end of myself. I was sure I would die soon. I literally felt like I was "being poisoned inside". Somehow, I knew the extreme pain and agony I **felt** inside was now translating into **physical** sickness and death. I could not explain it. I just "knew it", though I knew almost nothing at the time about how our physical bodies are affected by our emotional, mental or spiritual state.

And even without this "evil foreboding" that I was becoming sick, I certainly knew that I had been suffering tremendously emotionally. Through much strife and contention, I felt I had become too wounded and could not bear it anymore. Even greater than that was the pain of losing the one I loved. And the fact that it seemed like there was nothing that could be done to change that was definitely more than I could bear.

This was the state of being that I found myself in prior to going to *Be In Health™*.

What I Consider the Greatest Revelations I Gained from Be In Health™

Prior to attending the one or two weeks of programs, *Be In Health™* recommends that the person should read Pastor Henry's book, "***A More Excellent Way***", which covers many of the Scriptural insights that Pastor Henry has received, the related teachings from the Word of God and detailed information about the physiology of many sicknesses and diseases. It also introduces the reader to how Pastor Henry arrived at all this, lays out the foundations in the Word of God and includes several testimonies from people that have been healed through the ministry.

To be honest, I had no clue of what I was going to find in the book or at *Be In Health™*. In fact, I somewhat thought that all this was not going to apply too directly to my real situation because I was not physically sick, or at least, not yet anyway.

But, I was quite certain that I had heard from the Lord when He said "*...and go for two weeks*".

So, I scheduled to go and began to read the book.

As I began to read the book, I soon realized some things beyond the "sickness and disease thing".

The first few things I realized were that:

- there were **many Scriptures**; not just a few;
- the book would state and assert things which I saw as being "safely *within*", and *not "slightly outside"* of those Scriptures; and
- followed a pattern of giving those Scriptures *right after the statements and assertions.*

I realized the approach was actually connecting Scriptures with Scriptures and essentially **the assertions stated were clearly echoed by Scriptures**. In other words, he was not going "beyond the Scriptures" with his assertions; the Scriptures *were not being "stretched" beyond what they truly said.* In fact, he seemed to simply be "restating" what the Scriptures said, which I actually found refreshing and "easy to entreat".

> **James 3:17 But the wisdom that is from above is first pure, then peaceable, gentle, [and] easy to be intreated, full of mercy and good fruits, without partiality, and without hypocrisy.**

And then came the two topics that struck me more than anything or even "the sickness and disease thing". These were what they refer to as "**spiritual realities**" and its related insight that they refer to as "**separation**".

Spiritual Realities and Separation

You see, I thought of myself as a "spirit-filled believer", even a "Pentecostal" or "charismatic" believer as well, for lack of better terms. Therefore, I thought I knew about "spiritual warfare". I had a "classic church training" in those topics as taught in most churches. And I did know a few things.

But what I was missing was **a clearer understanding** about **what happens when people wrong us**. I read the part where Pastor Henry discussed the fact that **we tend to join or "make one" the person that wrongs us with the wrongs**. We associate **the person with all the anger, bitterness, resentment and other things that can come at us** from that person. We "blame the person" for what they have done to us. And because we see the person as the "guilty party", we also get the aforementioned thoughts and feelings **about them and against them**.

I certainly could identify with that part of what he described. I loved...**and** yet **I also had "negative feelings" about the persons** that had hurt me and wronged me. But as I continued reading what Pastor Henry was sharing, I began to see **the "separation"** between the person made of "flesh and blood" and what he and the Scriptures tell us that we are actually wrestling against, which we have looked at since the beginning of this book.

> **Ephesians 6:12 For we wrestle not against flesh and blood, but against principalities, against powers, against the rulers of the darkness of this world, against spiritual wickedness in high [places].**

As I read the Scriptures and Pastor Henry's explanations that **distinguished** between the **spiritual** enemies and the **physical** "enemies", I began to see that difference more clearly and began to "separate" the persons from the "negative things" that had come against me through the persons.

I sensed the anointing of the Holy Spirit working and giving me personal revelation and insight as I read those things. I also sensed <u>a certain amount of relief</u> and <u>a loosening of the grip</u> that those "negative thoughts and feelings" had **on me** and **against the persons of flesh and blood.**

But the real breakthrough and release came on the first day of actual teachings at *Be In Health*™.

My whole world began to open up when I heard a phrase there that I will never forget. It was as if all sound stopped when the speaker on the session on "spiritual realities" said "fear is not just an emotion".

That phrase, for some reason, hit me like a ton of bricks and got my attention.

I immediately asked myself and the Holy Spirit: "What do you mean? Of course it is an emotion!" And instantly, the Holy Spirit said to me: "He did not say fear was **not an emotion** but that it was *not JUST* an emotion".

Oh. So I asked myself: "Well, ***what ELSE*** is it then?"

Friends, that statement and my question to it began an absolute floodgate of personal revelation! The Holy Spirit opened up to me thing after thing after thing that I had not understood as clearly before!

From that moment on, He spoke to me all the while the speakers were teaching on the various topics. It was incredible even for me, who was "used to" hearing the Lord speak to me and show me many things. It was flowing so freely that I filled one and a half composition notebooks in those two weeks alone!

And, I was having to work very hard to keep up with writing all the insights that the Holy Spirit was giving me right along with the notes I was taking from the teachers! I remember my hand hurting often and rubbing and shaking it during the spurts of revelation...and I am used to writing a lot!

It was hard but also wonderful at the same time!

But what came together in my spirit soon after that statement about fear was absolutely and unequivocally life-changing for me!

Though I had not been particularly oppressed by fears in my life, that statement about fears immediately helped me realize that **things I had thought were "just emotions" all my life, even as a Christian, _were much more than "just emotions"_. _What else_** were they? They were **"spirits of"**! Spirits of what? **Spirits of...whatever the emotion was!**

Just like fear came from "the spirit of fear", I suddenly saw and knew with certainty that emotions did not come "from nowhere" or from "situations". They were coming from spirits! Living beings!

> **2 Timothy 1:7 For God hath not given us the spirit of fear; but of power, and of love, and of a sound mind.**

It all came together, as has been explained more clearly in earlier chapters. I saw, for the first time in my walk as a born-again, spirit-filled believer that:

- Thoughts do not just "float in the air"
- Thoughts come from "a mind"
- Therefore only "some**one**" could have, and give, thoughts
- The same held true for "emotions": only **a living being** could have them and give them!

Oh, HalleluYah! That was then, and is still now (as I write this at 5 in the morning) so very exciting and liberating! Why?

Because I realized that all those tormenting thoughts and feelings I was suffering with, and being tormented by, were not coming "from my situation". I had become blinded in my situation. I was being made to think **like it was inevitable that I had to feel that way.** It "**seemed only right**" that I **would feel in a way that matched my situation.**

Because I was in a <u>depressing</u> and <u>sad</u> **situation** that seemed <u>hopeless</u>, **I was depressed and sad and feeling desperately hopeless**...and had *__no thought of fighting it!__*

And the next realization was just as powerful*: __it was not of God for me to feel these feelings, think those thoughts... it was other spirits...evil spirits...attacking me!__*

Friends, **that was the beginning of my freedom right there**! It may seem obvious now by this point of the book, and it may seem obvious to some, **but you'd be amazed at how many of your believing friends might not realize that all those "negative thoughts and feelings" they wrestle with are actual, bona fide "spirits** of the evil kind", for there is nothing holy about them!

The reason I was being literally "squashed" day by day was that I was being oppressed and tormented by these wicked, evil spirits, constantly and progressively, **and had no idea of this fact.**

And this was the worst thing: I was not doing anything to try to remove them or get rid of them because I did not fathom that I could!

The best anyone had done, from many well-meaning pastors, counselors and friends, was to tell me what to do and what not to do; what to feel and think and what not to feel and think...but I could not do it!

I thought it was "inevitable" and "because of my situation". **And, all along, it was evil spirits!**

Had I known that, I would have come against those spirits in the Name above all names!

And yet, the model I had learned about traditional "spiritual warfare" was not as effective or powerful as the model that *Be In Health*™ practiced upon the group and taught us to use for the rest of our life and walk. Interestingly, this model was also much simpler and obvious than the one I had learned, which is still very prevalent in most churches and congregations today, **which miss the whole issue of separation and recognition of the spiritual realities mentioned above**.

I know this because, as we progressed through these topics during that first week at *Be In Health*™, they would lead us, as a group, through the following basic steps (we will look at these steps in greater detail in the next chapter):

1. **RECOGNIZE** that all these "negative thoughts and emotions" were coming from evil spirits, both against me through others but also through me against others;
2. take **RESPONSIBILITY** for such participation; and then
3. **REPENT** for the sin of **participating and/or believing the lies** instead of God's Truth; then
4. **RENOUNCE** further **agreement and participation** with such evil, ungodly beings.

Once these 4 steps were accomplished, ONLY THEN would they move on to the 5th and decisive step, which is to:

5. **REMOVE**, in which they would now command, in the Name of Jesus/Yeshua, the evil spirits which were the owners and culprits of those emotions and thoughts to come out and leave us.

And you know what? They left! We knew because the thoughts and emotions would leave. Depression, sadness, hopelessness and grief left! HalleluYah!

And you know what was left? "Things" like peace...joy...faith...the opposite of torment, sadness and hopelessness!

As "other spirits" left, then only the Holy Spirit was left and His fruit was now evident and manifest! (Recall that this was discussed in Chapter 5.)

We hasten to present here that an important part of this 5th step is to have our minds renewed by the Truth in the Word of God, so as to learn to act in accordance with the Word and, for example, not agree again with the patterns of thinking or the lessons that we have been taught by, say, spirits of fear. We must break the long-term habits and memories created by incorrect thinking patterns that are not in accordance with the Word of God and then replace them with ways of thinking that are in accordance with the Word. If we do not do this also, we will remove the spirits but they can then return if we were to again agree with them and be led of them. We must simply learn to not be led by them once we have learned to recognize them and have removed them through the above steps. In other words, we must learn to **resist** them, which is the next "maintenance step".

6. **RESIST** simply means that we now purpose to walk in agreement with the way the Word tells us to think and agree only with the Word. Thus, we do not allow ourselves to be led or moved by the evil spirits that formerly taught us to think, feel and act in ways opposite to the Word. We take every thought captive and bring them to the obedience of Christ (2 Corinthians 10:5).

As the sessions, topics and days went by, we could all notice ourselves, and others, looking and feeling better, being freer to worship God unhindered, sleeping better, etc. We all felt like modern-day examples of the Gadarene demoniac discussed in Chapter 3. We were all realizing we were more and more "sitting at the feet of Yeshua in our right minds"!

HalleluYah!

We were all realizing more clearly that the Word of God was still true, even today, just as it was when the Messiah walked the earth! His power was still the same today! His Name still "worked" like it did then! We realized that nowhere does the Bible tell us that evil spirits were no more...or that "they could not bother us when we become Christians".

I also realized that most of the people that say that "a Believer cannot have an evil spirit once they are born again" are the very people that display these same "negative thoughts and feelings" and are just as unaware, as I was, that such are caused by evil spirits.

I now realize that only because:

- I heard the Truth of God's Word taught in a simple and fresh way
- It was stated plainly
- under the power and anointing of the Holy Spirit
- I was open to teaching and knowledge
- I was teachable
- I did not reject knowledge
- I desired, and needed, to be changed by Him,
- I repented and allowed Him to show me

- I trusted Him to deliver me and set me free
- He delivered me from destruction and captivity!

Pastor Henry's desire is to simply see the same deliverance from all those that are oppressed of the devil. It was always God's desire as well.

> **Acts 10:38 How God anointed Jesus of Nazareth with the Holy Ghost and with power: who went about doing good, and healing all that were oppressed of the devil; for God was with him.**

Those that deny or refuse to examine that these spirits still work on us as described do not allow themselves to go through the items listed above...and so they **continue displaying fruit like irritability, impatience, resentment, bitterness, accusations, criticism, pride**...as well as "the other end of the spectrum": **sadness, loneliness, feeling rejected and unloved, unworthiness, shame, guilt, condemnation, depression, discouragement, etc.**

Having experienced how this has made all the difference, it is now also, more than ever, one of my greatest desires: to help the hurting and struggling believers be set free from all the afflictions of the enemy and his army. *This passion burns within me more than ever.*

The insights and understanding He gave me during those two weeks in 2005 have only continued to increase and become clearer and deeper as I have continued walking with Him. **I continue to see and understand more and more *as He shows me greater understanding through many situations.***

Since then, I have personally seen scores of brothers and sisters in the Lord, *whom it has been my privilege and honor to serve and minister to*, benefit greatly from these insights and practical **application of God's Word.**

It is nothing more than following the example that Yeshua demonstrated for us. He said to go and heal the sick, cleanse the lepers, raise the dead and cast out devils as we went and that in so doing, the Kingdom of God would come upon us.

> **Matthew 10:8 Heal the sick, cleanse the lepers, raise the dead, cast out devils: freely ye have received, freely give.**

> **Luke 11:20 But if I with the finger of God cast out devils, no doubt the kingdom of God is come upon you.**

Now that I've shared with you a little bit about *Be In Health*™ and how God did such a wonderful and mighty work in me and in others through these insights, let me share with you in the next chapter some practical steps to help us bring together all of the insights we have learned so far in this study.

We will now help the reader "put it all together" so it can help you **remove the enemy that we have been learning to recognize.**

Having recognized them...let us now remove them!

10

HAVING RECOGNIZED...
LET US REMOVE!

Now that we have discussed in detail the truths and principles from the Word of God that are involved in the struggle that we are in, let us start wrapping up this study **by putting our insights into practical steps and application**.

As promised since the introduction of this book, **the whole purpose and objective of this study is to remove the enemy and his army**, from **our own lives first**, and **then** from **the lives of so many others that are afflicted of this invisible army**. But in order to remove him, we first had to **learn how to recognize this army** *and separate this spiritual enemy from our flesh-and-blood brethren!*

We also had to **learn to stop believing that these "negative things" were just** *"our sinful nature"* **or** *"our flesh"*.

Once we do that, we can **"see the real enemy" anytime we encounter them**, whether against us in our own lives or in the lives of others.

And **now that we see the real enemy**, we can now begin to fight **the real battle...**"with our **eyes really open**".

Now we can **stop fighting flesh and blood** people. **Now** we don't get blindly caught up into **blaming people, as if we wrestled flesh and blood**. Now we realize we battle *evil, spiritual enemies.* And **now**, we recognize them when we see them.

Recognizing the True Enemy Must Precede True Deliverance

We must *first* be awakened to the fact that "true deliverance" must first involve properly discerning ungodly thoughts, feelings, emotions, attitudes, urges, actions and even "philosophies and theologies" (1 Timothy 4:1) as the work of evil spirits...since those can **never** be **the work of the Holy** Spirit.

Many deliverance ministries, pastors and ministers deal with some of the more "definable spirits", such as those of lust, perversion, addictions, etc. **But far too many completely overlook fears, anxieties, worries, anger, bitterness, unforgiveness, grief, *ungodly* sorrow, depression, hopelessness, and others as simply "the circumstances", "character flaws" or "immature believers". They just "counsel" people**. Sadly, the spirits behind those thoughts, feelings and impulses "stay warm and cozy in the host" right through those "counseling sessions", often for years!

And, all the while, the enemy and his army laugh at the ignorance and spiritual blindness of the poor, afflicted and often dying believers as well as at the ignorance and blindness of the counselors, pastors and ministers.

Practical Steps for Recognizing the Enemy...Even In Ourselves

Since we have learned in earlier chapters to recognize what the Spirit of God is like in us - in thought, word and deed - versus the "works of the flesh" (the work of the intelligent, purposeful and willful **"dwellers of the flesh"**), it should almost be easy for us now to recognize when the enemy is at work in or through us by checking a few things.

Step One: Check Your Thoughts

One of the best ways to identify and recognize the enemy is by asking, yourself or others, a question such as:

- **"What am I / are you thinking?"**

As we learned, **thoughts do not just "float around"** and **cannot exist apart from somebody's mind.** Only a mind can generate thoughts. And anything with a mind is not a thing: it is "a living, intelligent being".

And **that being can be visible** but "it" **can also be invisible**.

Would you recognize if an invisible being is giving thoughts to a visible being? (Remember Peter in Matthew 16:16-17 and 16:22-23.)

1. **Realize** that the **thoughts and conclusions** of man **can come from God, and be in accordance with God.**

2. And most of us realize that we also can generate our own thoughts. Absolutely. We can have "our own thoughts".

3. **The question is, *do we also and equally*, realize that the enemy and his army can and do, and love to, plant thoughts into us?**

Thoughts to do that which is holy are brought by God **before we make them "our own".**

We learn that we are supposed to love, forgive and be patient and kind. We **did not "originate" nor "create" those thoughts or those teachings**. *We learned them from God at some point before* we learned to make them "our own thoughts" and "our own way".

Then, why is it so hard for us to realize that, *equally and conversely*, thoughts to do that which is un-holy and evil...are also **not "originated" nor "created" by us?**

Before such thoughts ever became "our own", they came from outside us! **We learned them from evil beings at some point** before we "agreed with those thoughts" and before they "seemed right" to "us".

Again, this does **not** free us from **responsibility** for sin...it only frees us from **the blame and condemnation for** the **origination** and **authorship** of sin. And it frees us up to disagree with, and then truly "put away", sin.

The first and greatest example was in the Garden of Eden.

Adam and Eve had learned to not eat from the tree of the knowledge of good and evil. They learned that from God! They did not "originate those teachings nor thoughts" of obeying God on their own.

But along came a living being, sin-ful and evil and intelligent...**and shared the thoughts of doing the opposite to what God said and taught**. That same being then **went further** and **cast doubt on what God had said**. The being **went further and gave "reasons", "justified" and "explained why it was OK" to go against what God said, taught and ordered!**

And so came the first act of *dis*-obedience. It was **<u>instigated by</u>** an evil, intelligent being...who was the enemy of God and His people and His creation. **And by that one dis-obedience by one man, sin (an army of sinful, living beings that do and did what we and Paul did not want to do) entered** into the world you and I live in:

> **Romans 5:12 Wherefore, as by one man sin entered into the world, and death by sin; and so death passed upon all men, for that all have sinned:**

That same being continued that same enterprise ever since unto this day: instigating disobedience by ***first, making us think his thoughts*** <u>(as though they were "our own" is most effective)</u> *and* ***then agreeing,*** *and* ***then acting against God's orders!***

Therefore, we realize now that:

- Thoughts, *__before they can be "our own thoughts__"*, were **learned** and **came** *from either* **God or his enemy and his army.**
- Thoughts are either in agreement with God's Word, God's truth and His principles, commandments, statutes and decrees...or they are in disagreement.
- Thoughts that disagree with God's Word, Truth and His commandments, statutes and decrees...come from the enemy and his army...since the beginning...and **even until now**.

Realize that thoughts **will seek to lead you either into obeying and acting in accordance with God...or will serve only to lead and guide you into dis-obeying God and acting in disagreement with God's Word and His ways.**

There is no "middle ground".

This is a powerful and yet simple way to discern *"who gave you those thoughts?"*

Step Two: Check Your Feelings

Another powerful and simple way to recognize the enemy is through checking your feelings.

Ask yourself (or others):

- **What am I/are you feeling?**
- **How am I/are you feeling?**

The answer will tell.

If you are feeling *love, joy, faith, patience, peace* and similar feelings, chances are that they are coming from the Holy Spirit within you and flowing through your life.

But, if instead, you feel "things" *like fear, worry and anxiety*, realize that the Word of Truth calls fear "the spirit of fear" (2 Timothy 1:7) and that the Word cautions us to be anxious for nothing and to fret not.

Therefore, I submit to you that **such "feelings" do not come from the Spirit of God... but from "other spirits".**

Remember that these are **not "*just* emotions".**

Remember that the first record in God's Word of "negative emotions" occurred in the Garden. Adam hid because he "was afraid" in Genesis 3.

Realize that 2 Timothy 1:7 reveals that God has not given us *the spirit of* fear.

Adam was also "ashamed". I submit to you that this *shame* was also not the fruit of the Holy Spirit. It was the fruit of "another spirit", like unto the spirit of fear.

We could say that "**positive emotions**", like love, joy and peace, **come from God**, Who is **a Spirit and a living being**. Likewise, realize that all "**negative emotions**" come from a living, spiritual being as well...but not a godly being but rather, an *unholy and evil* spirit being.

Now, someone might say *"the reason"* that Adam feared and was ashamed is that he was naked.

This is an example of what I call **"matching thoughts and feelings"**. As we have discussed, these are used together by our enemies to get us to think and believe "the reason" or "the justification" for **accepting the fruit of their presence** (thoughts and feelings especially) as "the truth" and that *"I can't help but feel this way because of the situation"*.

Let me illustrate how this deception works and how this is actually **"BUI"**: **"being under the influence" of evil spirits**.

- A person who is "worried" does not realize that such worry does not come from God. They "just think" that their worry **"cannot be helped because of the 'worrisome' situation"**.
- A person under the influence of a spirit of fear does not realize the fear comes from a spirit: they just think that they cannot help being fearful **because of "the reason** for their fear".
- A "bitter person" does not think there is anything wrong with their bitterness, because they are **also convinced** that **the bitterness they feel is "justified"**.

But the **Truth** is that:

- **No situation is worrisome to God Almighty**!
- **No situation is so threatening** that it causes **the Spirit of God in us to fear,** nor to tell us to fear. (His Word so often says *"fear not"*.)

- And **nothing that is ever done to us is "justification" to cause the "God in us" to feel bitterness** against another human being.

We are supposed to be **one with God's Spirit and God's feelings**...and **not** be one with the thoughts or feelings **of any other** spirit.

Step Three: Check What You Desire, Want or "Feel Like Doing"

Another great way to discern what (or who) might be influencing us is to check our desires, wants or what we "feel like doing".

This is because the Holy Spirit **will never "want to do", "feel like doing" or bring "the urge to"** do anything contrary to the Word of God, nor lead us with "reasons" to not follow or obey His Word.

For example, have you ever heard a believer say "*I felt like hitting that person*" or "*I wanted to smack that guy!*"? Have they also said "*my flesh wanted to hit him!*"?

I can assure you that **it was not the Holy Spirit that wanted to do that**. "Something" certainly did. But we have already established, and we now see clearly, that **only a living being can have "wants"**. **Wants imply desires and also decisions, reasoning and motives.**

Therefore, those people that say the above or similar things are **not being led or influenced by the Holy Spirit, nor the unthinking "flesh"**. There's a living, thinking, deciding, reasoning being with motives, **seeking to move that person to do such un-holy acts**. We can safely conclude that there is "another spirit" working through those persons and **not the Spirit of Messiah**.

> **Luke 9:54 And when his disciples James and John saw [this], they said, Lord, wilt thou that we command fire to come down from heaven, and consume them, even as Elias did?**
> **55 But he turned, and rebuked them, and said, Ye know not what manner of spirit ye are of.**
> **56 For the Son of man is not come to destroy men's lives, but to save [them]. And they went to another village.**

Step Four: Check Your Speech

Quite often, you do not even have to ask people anything. You will hear them talking and **you will be able to discern if they are listening to "Radio God" or "Radio Devil"**.

Remember that out of the abundance of the heart, the mouth speaks.

> **Luke 6:45 A good man out of the good treasure of his heart bringeth forth that which is good; and an evil man out of the evil treasure of his heart bringeth forth that which is evil: for of the abundance of the heart his mouth speaketh.**

If people are talking about how they forgive others, see the best in people and do not hasten to conclude against a person, **they are displaying, and "manifesting", the Spirit of God and His love** in their handling of a particular situation.

Likewise, the opposite is true. If people are talking about how someone *"has gone too far"*, *"does not deserve forgiveness anymore"* or *"has done it to me too many times"*, we can be certain that such is not the Holy Spirit talking, manifesting, authoring or influencing those words, conclusions or decisions...**but rather a spirit of bitterness, resentment and/or unforgiveness. They are truly "manifesting another spirit"...***and most believers are undiscerning of this* **and think it's just plain "reasoning".**

The principle is essentially **the same for our speech** as for our **thoughts, feelings and desires:**

- **if a person is speaking in harmony with the Word of God, they are being led of the Spirit of God.**
- If they are **speaking opposite the principles and teachings of the Word of God, they are being led by** *another spirit* **or are speaking and manifesting** *the teachings* **of another spirit.**

Step Five: Check Your Actions

This is another great way to discern, and is direct and almost inescapable, as even those who do not discern the spirits behind the scenes, and "blame the people themselves" for the actions, cannot deny that deeds are the final result, or outworking, of whatever is working "within or upon the person".

Checking our acts or deeds certainly sheds light on what, **or who**, is influencing us, just like the four aspects and steps above. **That's because acts and** deeds that are ungodly can never be said to be motivated by the Holy Spirit.

Therefore, again, **unholy deeds can only be** motivated, felt, thought, desired and **ultimately propelled by a living being of an un-holy sort**.

And yet, we still have some folks that deny the influence and work of evil spirits, <u>but they themselves exhibit unholy behavior and simply "blame their flesh" and their "fallen, sinful nature"</u>.

Thoughts, Feelings, Desires, Words and Deeds: Great Ways to "Check Ourselves"

Therefore, if we ask ourselves or others:

- **"What am I / are you <u>thinking</u>?"**
- **"What/How am I / are you <u>feeling</u>?"**
- **"What do I / you <u>want to do</u> or <u>feel like doing</u>?"**
- **"What do I / you <u>say or talk like</u>?**
- **"What do I / you <u>do or act like</u>?**

If the answers are "things" like feelings that do not match, or go against, the fruit of the Spirit, **chances are very high** that there is **"another spirit"** at work, having *its* **emotions "mixed in with yours"**...*and making you think that it is "natural" and that "it is you and your fallen, sinful, human nature"*.

Chances are also very high that you will have "***matching thoughts***" to those emotions: **"reasons" that conveniently "justify" the fact that you are** experiencing **"emotions" or "conclusions" about the situations** you are in.

And, the things you want to do, desire to do or feel like doing, and the resulting words and deeds, are likely going to be the result of, and also be "matching", the "thoughts and feelings" discussed above.

I say again, as we have seen in earlier chapters, that most Believers are not aware clearly enough of the fact that:

- Thoughts and feelings **only come from living beings.**
- Thoughts and feelings **other than those of the Holy Spirit and His fruit** must be coming from "other spirits" and not just "the flesh"...**but its "dwellers".**
- **Urges or "desires to do" also only come from living beings.**
- **Speech and actions are the same way: they come from living beings.**
- These other spirit beings influence us, and often hide and dwell, in our bodies or flesh...*and make us think that it is "us" or "our flesh" that is the problem.*

We must realize, and cannot reject that, Scripturally, "the flesh" at the very least includes "**the sin that dwells in** the flesh" (Romans 7:17-20) and that **it is the same sin that entered** by one man (Romans 5:12).

Step Six: Check Your "State of Mind": Where Do The Thoughts and Feelings Leave You?

Now that you have checked your thoughts, feelings, desires **and even the resulting outward speech**, also ask yourself: <u>**in what "state of mind" do those thoughts and feelings leave you, even if you do not act them out or say them**</u>?

Do you feel:

- Encouraged?
- Loved?
- Satisfied with yourself?
- Others? God? Your house/car? Your life?
- **At peace**?

Or, do your thoughts and feelings <u>seem to support, or be based upon</u>, "facts" **that then make you feel**:

- Restless?
- Confused?
- Dissatisfied?
- In conflict with something/one??
- Inferior?
- Unworthy?
- Undeserving?
- Guilty?
- Ashamed?
- Defective?
- At fault?
- To blame?
- Angry (at others, or yourself)?
- Bitter?

- Resentful ("sore" at people)?
- Hateful?
- Sad?
- Depressed?
- Lonely?
- Alone?
- Abandoned?
- Defeated?
- Hopeless?
- Suicidal

The thing to remember at this point, no matter what the facts or the situation may be, is that **nothing is so "impossible" for God that "all is lost"**. There is *always* hope with God and **our loving and omnipotent Father** <u>can</u> and **does want to** do "the impossible" **to restore and improve our lives!**

> **Luke 1:36 And, behold, thy cousin Elisabeth, she hath also conceived a son in her old age: and this is the sixth month with her, who was called barren.**
> **<u>37 For with God nothing shall be impossible</u>.**
>
> **Matthew 17:20 And Jesus said unto them, Because of your unbelief: for verily I say unto you, If ye have faith as a grain of mustard seed, ye shall say unto this mountain, Remove hence to yonder place; and it shall remove; <u>and nothing shall be impossible unto you</u>.**

So, ask yourself: whatever is telling you that things are so bad, terrible, depressing and hopeless, or fearful and worrisome, **is it coming from God?** Is it "in agreement with God"? <u>Are those thoughts and feelings</u> **God's opinion** about your life's situations?

<u>Nothing</u> worries, confuses or surprises God. He will give you hope about anything. Nothing is "too much" for God.

Therefore, I submit to you that <u>those</u> "**negative thoughts and feelings**" **come from other living beings feeding you** *their* **perspective** about the situation, **instead of God's perspective, which is the only one that really matters, and which has the final say.**

Step Seven: Identify Them...and Make a List!

Now that you have checked the thoughts, feelings, desires and perhaps even any outward acts or speech, and have analyzed what state of mind all those thoughts and feelings leave you in, you should be able to identify the particular living beings, or spirits, that are responsible for doing that to you. You should be able to see who is, or are, acting upon you.

If you are experiencing "negative", ungodly thoughts, feelings, desires and states of being, then you must realize that ***those spirits*** "are doing a number on you". ***Those spirits*** are feeding you ***their*** thoughts and feelings, and urging you to act and speak, in ways that are not in accordance, nor in agreement with, God.

You can now realize that "these things" that you have been experiencing are **not the fruit of the Holy Spirit** in your life (Galatians 5:22-23) but **rather the evil fruit of unholy spirits** that want to do what you and Paul did not want to do (Romans 7). These **sinful,**

invisible spirits do not announce themselves, they act out **their** evil, sinful **natures** through you and me if we let them, *__and then tell us, your psychologist and your pastor that this is just "our sinful, fallen nature"__*.

They deceive us into all this, and they get away with blaming us as being "defective".

Beloved brethren, we are just vessels. Perhaps what is in us is sinful...but we ourselves are just "cups". We can "cleanse the vessel" and then fill it up with God's content.

Remember: we are to be God's temple. Therefore, let us remove every dweller from that temple that does not belong there and then the only "Dweller" that is supposed to live in us, the Holy Spirit, will have free reign to live, feel, think, desire, speak and act through us!

That is what Scriptures tell us is supposed to be our new life in Him. And, as we saw in Chapter 5, this is possible if we would just identify and remove anyone other than the Holy Spirit from us.

Step Eight: Decide If You Do Not Want These Beings Inside You

Now that you have realized that invisible, yet very real beings that are very wicked, evil, foul and unholy are coming against you, seeking to kill, steal and destroy all the good in your life and in the lives of others, **you've come to the brink of your breakthrough**.

You are not just going to **"make yourself do"** anything. You are **not** going to **"only control yourself"**. You are **not** going to **"make yourself"** not do something anymore.

Why? **Because those are not the situations you are in**. Because you know it is **not "you alone"** but rather, it is **them in and through you**, all you have to do is come **against them** and **get rid of them**. **Kick them out. Evict them**. *How?*

If you do make a quality decision that **you truly do not want to participate with** these evil beings, **nor *let them work their works*** through you, then you are going to avail yourself of the power, authority and "Helper" that God gave you and me and ***you are going to remove the enemy***.

You are going to cast out evil spirits...by the finger of God.

> **Luke 11:20 But if I with the finger of God cast out devils, no doubt the kingdom of God is come upon you.**

> **Matthew 12:28 But if I cast out devils by the Spirit of God, then the kingdom of God is come unto you.**

Armed with the understanding from His Word and His Truths that you have gained by this point, you can now go on to the step that we have been working towards all along in this study.

Now that we recognize the enemy, we can go on to remove the enemy!

Step Nine: Let Us Remove...Using "The 8 R's"

This section follows the pattern known as "the 8 R's" as taught by Pastor Henry Wright and *Be In Health*™. As mentioned in the acknowledgements section and elsewhere in this book, much of what is shared in this book has been adopted and learned from Pastor Henry's books, teachings and programs through the ministry that I have personally received in 2005, combined with the continuing personal revelations, insights and growth that I have been blessed to receive since.

In addition, I have been able to minister these revelations and insights to many since 2005 and the Father of all mercies works through these for the benefit of many who have been blessed, instructed, delivered, set free and healed as they cooperate and yield to the Holy Spirit of God in their lives and receive the anointed Word of God.

By the time you reach this point of the book, not much else needs to be explained, as most has been explained by now. Therefore, the 8 R's are now listed here with only a brief description of what is involved at each step.

Note that this is not meant to be a "formula" of any kind but rather a practical pattern of Scriptural principles to use God's model in applying the effectual Word of God to our lives and bring the deliverance from the forces of darkness, as God intends for us and as taught in the Scriptures.

1. RECOGNIZE

- Recognize and identify the ungodly, sinful being that is working his influence upon you or the person in need of ministry. By recognizing the unholy behavior, acts, thoughts, feelings or desires, you can identify that there is a corresponding being at work. Recognize the sin that is not pleasing to, nor approved by, God.

2. Take RESPONSIBILITY

- You realize that you must take action to "choose life" and "choose to obey" God's Word and will for your life; that you desire to obey the Holy Spirit and not any other spirits; that you can break the generational curses or iniquities that may have been passed to the 3rd and 4th generations, and that you will take the appropriate action in choosing to follow the paths of righteousness instead of the paths of destruction. You also acknowledge your past actions, that it is up to you alone to choose and you choose to act.

3. REPENT

- You must acknowledge your participation with sin before God; you choose to repent for such actions and to turn away from such actions.

4. RENOUNCE

- You renounce "your agreement" with the notions that you accepted about the sinful acts and you resolve to agree only with God's view on the subject. You decide that you agree with God's perspective and Word on the subject and you choose to conform to and accept God's Word on the matter instead of what others or the world might say.

5. REMOVE

- Now that you have repented for your sinful acts and have come out of and renounced your agreement with the evil, sinful, thinking beings that influenced you into their desires, you now break the power and take authority over those evil spirits, in the Name of Jesus Christ of Nazareth, and by the power of the Holy Spirit, you cast them out of you and remove them from your body, the temple of the Holy Spirit and out of your life. **You evict the evil spirits**.

6. RESIST

- Now that you have cleansed your temple and have driven off the unauthorized dwellers, you resolve to stay sober and vigilant and guard your mind and heart. You bring every thought captive to the obedience of Christ and you resist the devils and his army from influencing you again. When you do, and you are truly submitted to Him, they will flee from you when you resist and rebuke them.

7. REJOICE

- You are to be thankful to Him that delivered you from darkness into his marvelous light, offer up the sacrifice of praise and the fruit of our lips, praise Him in the midst of the congregation and give blessing, honor, glory and power unto Him that is worthy and deserving and you rejoice in the Lord.

8. RESTORE

- After we are strengthened, we are to strengthen our brethren; we are to pray one for another that we may be healed, and we are to freely give as we have freely received (Matthew 10:8).

Final Thoughts About Removing The Enemy

While each "R" reflects some solid and important Scriptural principles, you will come to realize that **the first five R's** are the most crucial in terms of removing the enemy from our lives. After **the groundwork is laid in the first four R's**, the spirits are **actually removed and cast out in the fifth R**. Once this happens, you will often notice a release and relief in the characteristics of the particular spirit(s) that you were removing. You will also usually feel more of the fruit of the Holy Spirit, in terms of peace and joy. Remember also that we must also renew our mind with the Truth of the Word and learn new thinking patterns that are in accordance with the Word and not with the spirits we remove. Remember that both aspects are crucial and work together.

The sixth R now becomes crucial in <u>maintaining the deliverance and peace</u> that comes from the removal of the tormenting, evil spirits. You must now be very careful to stay alert to notice if you sense the influence of evil trying to attack your thoughts or feelings in a clandestine attempt to bring you to its obedience instead of and against the Word of God in any unsanctified area of your life.

The seventh and eighth R's are then reflective of the attitude and consequence that our deliverance and freedom ought to bring and result in. We are to give Him thanks in all things, especially for his goodness, mercy and deliverance in our lives. And, now that we are free to serve Him better, we are better able to go forth and help and comfort others in the consolation and deliverance that we have received ourselves, for now we know how to effectively defeat those situations that once held us captive.

Benefits and Results of Removing the Enemy

As stated before and mentioned in the introduction, removing the enemy removes the influence of unholy spirits from our lives and leaves us **more free and unhindered to serve the Lord more fully**. We are **freer to have Him be the only One who indwells, leads, guides and moves through us**. We are **free to have His mind and His alone thinking through us**. We experience His peace, love and personality more fully in our own lives. He can flow more fully in and through us towards others. His love, mercy and compassion can operate without opposition or "interference" from other "thoughts or feelings" that come from spirits that oppose His work, actions and decisions.

It also becomes **"easier to hear Him"** and sense Him within us. It becomes **easier to become one with**

Him and yield ourselves to Him. We all can **experience a deeper level of fellowship and of His presence** in us. This has **far reaching effects** that have to be experienced to be believed!

As described in Chapter 9, even during and after the group deliverance sessions at *Be In Health*™ in 2005, I could literally feel the release from the torments and unrest and also feel the increase of the peace, serenity and joy that come from being surrounded by Him and not by other spiritual forces that so many, even believers, are afflicted by every day. I began to feel like I was experiencing what the Gadarene demoniac felt when, as Scripture says, he was suddenly able to sit at the feet of Yeshua in his right mind. HaleluYah for His goodness, power and deliverance!

My prayer, and the whole intention of this book, is *that every believer may have the eyes of their understanding enlightened, come to know the truth of God in these areas in a deeper way, as the Spirit brings revelation, and may then have those truths truly set them free.*

That way, **we become the holy, sanctified and powerful army that God wants us to be, which does not lack love, health or power** to **do the works of Yeshua, be a light unto a dark world, and take authority over the powers of darkness,** as Yeshua did, and walk in authority and heal the sick and deliver all those that are oppressed of the devil and his army!

11

SUMMARY AND EPILOGUE...
FOR NOW

Now that we have discussed all these things...what more can be said to you? What more shall I say to you?

Let me sum up the message of this book, and my message to you, the reader, in this way.

This message is about what your problems, and what my problems, and the problems of any believer, really are...**and what the problems really are not.**

What The Problem Really Is

Your problem is not "the flesh", as most believers understand it.

As we have seen, the problem is really "**what dwells or lives**" in the flesh. We have seen that the "sin that dwells in the flesh" entered by one man...**and has been disturbing the life of man on earth ever since.**

The Body of sin, which is the opposite of "the Body of Messiah", is composed of **an army of spirits that**

are invisible and evil. They have been **manifesting their nature, and their evil plans and purposes for man (to steal, kill and destroy) ever since the fall** in the Garden of Eden.

Those plans and purposes are those of their "commander-in-chief", Satan (HaSatan in Hebrew).

We must realize that, **though we live in, and were born into this physical world without the knowledge of these "spiritual realities"** discussed in this book, **we are spiritual beings. We were created by Yahweh, Who is a Spirit** (John 4:24).

He **also created the physical world** we live in today. And **He gave us physical bodies** to move around and live **in this physical world.**

And He also gave us **a soul**: a **mind, emotions,** a **will** and **senses** with which to sense, process and understand this physical world...as well as the spiritual things.

We must also remember that all things that are seen were created by things that are not seen (Hebrews 11:3).

Knowing this clearly, we must remember that, once upon a time, all things, spiritual and physical, were beautiful, wonderful, perfect, and there were no "problems". All created spiritual beings were subjected to, obeyed, and worshipped their Creator, and rightly so.

Therefore, all things were perfect and wonderful, just as He is Perfect and Wonderful.

But, somewhere in time, one spiritual being rebelled, iniquity being found in him, and pride leading him to rebel and seek a place higher than that appointed to him, though he was appointed to much, and sought to be exalted to a place set only for the Most High. He lost in his attempt, **and was cast down** to earth, **to this physical world**, and to its atmosphere, **yet in spirit form**, *along with those spirit beings that he led in rebellion.*

And then, one day, in the garden, according to Genesis 3 and Romans 5:12, they – this kingdom of darkness, this body of sin, this "sin" problem – entered into this world.

Once this man, the first Adam, yielded himself to sin, he became its (his/their) servant (Romans 6:16)...**and ever since, sin has dwelled in the flesh** (Romans 7:17-20).

We have to remember, understand and be very clear about this. Because then, we can see what it really meant when, about four thousand years later, another man, "the last Adam", walked this physical world. And this man, Yeshua our Messiah, walked the earth **and undid what Adam did. He recovered what Adam lost**. He **fixed the damage that resulted from Adam's error and what Adam spoiled!**

What exactly did Yeshua do? Though much has been said, taught and preached about this, let me put it in very simple but powerful terms.

Yeshua fixed *the* problem. The only problem that there ever really was: *the root of all other*

problems. But then again, **it was not a problem that the Almighty, the Omniscient, the Wonderful One, was ever without a perfect solution to.** He brought His "Solution" in the fullness of time.

The problem was that man, Yahweh's creation, had erred and thus **contaminated himself, *and his seed*, with a spiritual intruder**. That spiritual intruder, and his army of beings, entered man ever since. **And began, and continue to this day, to manifest *their* nature, thoughts, plans, acts and deeds, through sinful-being-contaminated mankind.**

THAT is "the problem".

This problem was evident from the instant after the first disobedience, and from the very next generation from Adam and Eve. Sin was "crouching at the door" and Cain murdered Abel. The murderer was manifested (John 8:44).

Between Genesis 3 and Genesis 6, this problem was so bad that the intruders that entered by one man had so contaminated man that Yahweh saw the evil was continual in their hearts and decided to "start over". Realize that **the problem was not inherent to man**; it was **in man** but it was **not created nor propelled by** man. Yes, it was man's fault and decision **when deceived...but it was done upon man by an enemy**! **Yahweh's enemy! Our enemy! My enemy! Your enemy!** (1 Peter 5:8.)

He and his army have been carrying out his plan, this evil plan, **ever since sneaking through Adam and Eve**. We must "wake up" and see this...and know it, with every ounce of our being. For this is the Truth. His Word assures us of **these "facts of history", the history of one of Yahweh's creations known as "mankind".**

This "invisible problem" <u>continued</u> in man <u>even after the Flood</u>. Not all of Noah's children followed after YHVH. And so, man fell prey to the same contamination that **was not washed away nor drowned away by the physical waters** of the Flood. **That same evil, that same spiritual contamination of evil, <u>invisible beings</u>, continued to work through mankind.**

It was still evident as it manifested through all the pagan nations and peoples...and even through the lives and children of the Patriarchs. **It was still evident and present** through the children of Jacob/Israel, both **through his sons** against Joseph, **and in the tribes that descended from** his sons.

The children of Israel displayed the struggle **within man** (but **not _of_ man**) all through the wilderness experiences. And, even after that whole wicked and evil generation that tempted YHVH all those ten times perished in the desert according to His Word and judgments (except for Joshua and Caleb), the evil was **also not removed from man through the physical death.** It was **still evident** as that generation entered and took the Promised Land through Joshua. The Book of Judges shows that clearly.

The rest of the Bible bears out the continuation of wickedness and all manner of evil, both in thoughts, feelings, acts and deeds.

And then, that man came along: the "last Adam". And He began to show mankind and all the inhabitants of this physical earth what man's struggle was really all about.

How Yeshua Demonstrated "The Real Problem"

Again, though much has been said, taught and preached about what Yeshua accomplished on the earth, and what He demonstrated, I submit that we, as the Body of Believers, have still not fully realized what He actually showed us.

He did show us many, many things. He Himself taught us the Word of Yahweh. He Himself was the Word of YHVH that took on the form of physical man, and dwelt among us. It is marvelous!

And yet, perhaps the greatest thing He demonstrated to us was that we were **spiritually blind**...because we dealt with **everything physical**...as if it was all determined by, and therefore only solvable by, *physical remedies, methods and solutions*.

But He showed us otherwise.

First of all, do we not remember how they were amazed when He commanded unclean spirits out of a man (at a synagogue, no less) and "it" (they) obeyed Him?

> **Mark 1:23 And there was in their synagogue a man with an unclean spirit; and he cried out,**

24 Saying, Let [us] alone; what have we to do with thee, thou Jesus of Nazareth? art thou come to destroy us? I know thee who thou art, the Holy One of God.
25 And Jesus rebuked him, saying, Hold thy peace, and come out of him.
26 And when the unclean spirit had torn him, and cried with a loud voice, he came out of him.
27 And they were all amazed, insomuch that they questioned among themselves, saying, What thing is this? what new doctrine [is] this? for with authority commandeth he even the unclean spirits, and they do obey him.

And it was "bad enough" (*for the enemy and his army, that is*) when He did this to unclean spirits that were afflicting people...**but then He also** showed His power over, *and* **the presence of evil *in*,** "the elements"!

Mark 4:39 And he arose, and rebuked the wind, and said unto the sea, Peace, be still. And the wind ceased, and there was a great calm.
40 And he said unto them, Why are ye so fearful? how is it that ye have no faith?
41 And they feared exceedingly, and said one to another, What manner of man is this, that even the wind and the sea obey him?

Luke 8:24 And they came to him, and awoke him, saying, Master, master, we perish. Then he arose, and rebuked the wind <u>and the raging of</u> the water: and they ceased, and there was a calm.
25 And he said unto them, Where is your faith? And they being afraid wondered, saying one to another, What manner of man is this! for he commandeth even the winds and water, and they obey him.

As pointed out before in earlier chapters, notice that the account in Luke 8:24 reveals that He rebuked the raging of the water, and not the water in and of itself, even though YHVH gave man power over the earth, and all things in it, and commanded to subdue it, and have dominion over it.

Then, Yeshua demonstrated also (as shown earlier in this book in more detail) that many sicknesses and diseases were caused directly by the presence of evil spirits of either infirmities or specific conditions, including spinal curvatures, the palsy, epilepsy, fevers, being blind, deaf, mute and many other conditions and situations. He even rebuked the fever in Peter's mother-in-law (Luke 4:39) and "it" left her.

The healings of those instances always included His dealing with, *and removing*, those evil spirits.

Beloved brethren**, if He demonstrated and taught us to remove the enemy...shouldn't we also? Does He not want us to also? Did He not command us to?**

We need to make sure that we remember that, while medical science is very good at *diagnosing what is wrong* in our physical bodies and systems, it usually does not know *why* something goes wrong. They can measure all manner of dysfunction...but they often do not know why it went wrong...nor can they reverse and fix the "root cause". Medical science itself admits that it is mostly "managing what it detects" and seeks to counteract what is happening...but rarely does it truly restore health, reverse or "cure" the root cause of a malfunction.

As discussed in Chapter 9, much of what is incurable and unknown as to the root cause is actually a result that shows in the physical body...but is the effect from **emotional and spiritual issues** that inevitably control, by our design and physiology, various **biological, chemical, endocrine and neurological pathways to our physical bodies, functions and health.**

We also touched on the fact that, by removing the spiritual enemies that bring "thoughts and feelings" that result in physical diseases, thousands of people with these "incurable diseases" are being restored to the health that our Good Father intended for us.

Therefore, I again submit that **"physical diseases" are not the real problem; just ramifications of the real problem.**

People Are Not "The Problem"...

We also saw in earlier chapters that people themselves are not the real problem. His Word tells us that we do not wrestle "flesh and blood".

The real problem are those principalities, powers, rules of darkness and all manner of spiritual, *not physical,* **wickedness!**

These powers, principalities, rulers and spiritual wickedness are intelligent and think. **They have minds. They are evil. They are alive. "Dead things" are none of these**.

Our problem, as *physical* **mankind, is that these beings are** *invisible* **to the physical eyes.** And, as I have said to many brethren as I travel, ***these beings do not announce themselves.***

These evil spirits do not want us to be clear on the fact that they are the problem. They do not want us talking about them. They do not like me, or other ministers who are successfully helping believers "recover themselves" (2 Timothy 2:24-26), to talk about them. They do not want us focusing on them.

They say that very thing! "Oh, *you can't be focusing 'so much' on evil spirits.*" Well, I've learned their trick: they accuse us of "overdoing it"...<u>so that we will "under do it"</u>.

The answer to that libel is simple: I'm not trying to focus "*too much*" or "*so much*". **I'm just trying to focus on them "just the right amount", as I am supposed to, according to Scripture.**

Where does Scripture tell me to fear, hate my enemy, hold bitterness, or tell me that my enemy is a physical person? **Nowhere**. And where does it tell me about my enemy and my battle and my weapons being **not carnal but spiritual**? *Just about everywhere!*

I'll stop talking about evil spirits being behind all evil thoughts, feelings, acts and deeds <u>when I start seeing that we have a Biblically accurate understanding and perception about who our enemy is, according to 1 Peter 5:8, Ephesians 6:12 and the many Scriptures we examined earlier.</u>

I'll stop talking and teaching this truth when I stop hearing pastors, teachers and believers alike **blaming**

flesh-and-blood as if flesh and blood people <u>created un-holiness</u>. They see that holiness comes from Yahweh...***but have been literally deceived by our enemy's network into thinking that all unholiness comes from "that wicked person" only.***

The very people **infected with** the sin think it is "their sin" and do not realize that this sin is alive and dwells <u>in them</u>, **and works <u>through them</u>**, and tells them, and anyone who will listen, that the sin is a "***physical, carnal or psychological defect* <u>inherent to man</u>**"!

<u>I'm sorry, but this contradicts Scripture</u>. And it contradicts what Yeshua did, and taught. It is clear when we openly examine foundational Scriptures and events.

The evil is in them, yes...but it is not "***inherently*** them", nor "***from*** them". There ***is*** a "separation", a difference, that we must see here.

As I said before: **if we do not <u>create</u>** holiness, and can only yield <u>to it/Him</u>, and become one <u>with it/Him</u>, and **let it/Him work through us**...<u>why isn't the opposite also true</u>?

If we do not create holiness, why is it that we think we create un-holiness, wickedness and evil? ***<u>Who told us</u>*** we created evil and wickedness?

I perceive that "man" has been so associated with "evil", "wickedness" and "sin" that somewhere along the line, **the enemy** succeeded in "imprinting into us", **and deceiving us**, into **<u>forgetting that, in the very beginning, sin came from him, and through him, and by him!</u>**

But, I am very clear on the fact that it is he that "infected man". Scripturally, he entered with his army, and have dwelled in our flesh and/or have been influencing us ever since! As stated before, he and his army are the real problem. They are the sin...not us. It is them through us! We have to realize this if we are to go back to the same closeness and fellowship with Yahweh as we had in the Garden of Eden.

We have to see this distinction between "us" and "the source of evil", the one and his army, all of whom seek to, and often do, spread their evil through us! They work through *us*! But they are not *us*. And we are not *them*!

Why do we have to acknowledge, and accept, that we and others, just like Adam and Eve, might just be "caught in the snare" of **having it/evil/them, *which we do not create*, *in* us** and *working through* **us?**

Because if we do not, that enemy continues to use us, **and then blame us, for his evil.**

Just like there is **a difference between "us"** *and the Source of the Good and Holiness that works through us*, we have to see that **we are also just vessels, beings that will agree with, and yield ourselves *to, the Holy One...or to the un-holy-ones*.**

Do you see? **We must see!**

I asked myself recently: why do most believers easily see that all our holiness is from Him, and "**Him through us**", but so few seem to realize that the evil in them is <u>not their own</u>, but rather "evil ones through them"?

The answer came to me like this:

<u>God has not desired to conceal from us that it is He, and His Holiness, through the His Holy Spirit, that works through us, and that He desires us to agree with, and yield ourselves to, Him</u>.

<u>**However, the enemy and his army absolutely have desired to, and been highly successful in, concealing from us that it is he, and his army, and their evil and wickedness, that works through us, and that he and his army deceive us into agreeing with them, and yielding ourselves to them and their thoughts, feelings, plans and purposes**</u>.

In short, we let them manifest themselves through us! We allow them to use us as their <u>agents</u>...their <u>vessels</u>...their <u>instruments</u>.

None of us would ever want to admit to that...and yet it is true...**but we're hardly aware of it when it happens**.

The Purpose of This Book

That is why this book was written: **to help us see, in simple yet profound ways, that we either are led**

of the Holy Spirit...or of some other living spirit that is not the Holy Spirit. Period.

As stated in Chapter 5, if we truly were the temple **of only** the Holy Spirit, **only** His fruit would manifest. But since we often manifest "other fruit", which cannot possibly come from the Holy Spirit, we must be letting **some other spirit act from their hiding places**.

We need to recognize that...**not *to "blame the devil" for our actions*. No. We must do this only so we can then effectively find and remove *the real source* of the problem; the very ones *that influence us into* evil actions.**

We must identify, and then remove, the real problem, as we started to discuss in this chapter.

"Seek and destroy", if you will. **We MUST.** Why?

If we don't destroy the source spirits...*they will continue to destroy us*: destroy our personal peace (shalom), our minds, our thought life, our emotions, our very selves.

Then, they destroy **others through us** and destroy **our relationships with them**: at work, at the congregation of believers and at home. **They destroy and steal** our **jobs**, our **ministries**, our **spouses**, our **children**, our **parents and any other relationship that is dear** to us.

And, and at the same time, **our walk with our Maker is destroyed**. We become full of (spirits of) *fears, bitterness, grief, doubt, unbelief*, etc. We walk in disobedience to our Father, because our "thoughts and feelings" take over, and become "truth" to us, and lead us against what we know is God (2 Corinthians 10:4, 5), *though we "know the Scripture"*.

"Thoughts and feelings" hijack our minds, emotions...and actions. *Evil spirits, unannounced,* **lead us in the wrong thoughts, feelings and acts...which all result in disobedience,** *curses and death of all kinds* **in our lives.**

And last, or at the same time, **those "hijacked thoughts and feelings" result in the ruin of our chemical, biological and physiological functions...resulting in** *the diseases that ravage us* in the Body of Christ, and lead us to the end and the wages of our sins: death in the physical body as well.

This is how this hidden enemy and his army have been wrecking us. This is how they have been stealing from us, killing us...and destroying all they can.

As for me, brethren, I am now, more than ever, committed to rising from the ashes of my past failures and losses, and being a wiser instrument of the Captain of the Hosts, of being a more skilled soldier against our cunning enemy and his army. I am committed to what I have been called to do: to help strengthen my brethren and help them see the real enemy and the real army...and the real problem. And then, to help them yank the enemy out. Period.

"Co-habitating with the enemy" does not work. Bribing the enemy does not work. Appeasement and compromising do not work. He and his army absolutely are out to steal, kill and destroy...just as the Scriptures of Truth say. *The enemy absolutely will steal from us, like a schoolyard bully, as long as we let him.*

Well, I say he has bullied me **enough**. He has stolen **enough**. He ruined and stole perhaps the most precious finding in this life, up to now, besides the Lord...and my resolve is now galvanized to fight, fulfill my calling **and help the Body do the same: reach our individual, and corporate, "Promised Lands".**

My faith and trust is not in me...**but in the Omnipotent One Who dwells in me and has given me insights, "x-ray vision" and discernment like never before, on this side of pain, tears and sorrows. He has restored, refreshed and equipped.**

No more "dying in the wilderness". No more falling prey to fear of giants, no more doubting the Holy One because of "thoughts and feelings" that point to pharaohs or giants, or accuse YHVH of not providing enough water, or of providing light bread, or of not providing meat, **or any other unholy notion that disagrees with the Holy One.**

No more of *"being helpless to sin"* **due to the doctrine of "man's sinful nature"**, and how helpless we are to it. No more futile efforts to try to "control it". That is a losing proposition and a doctrine of the enemy. **No more of "we can never completely control sin"**! Scripture tells us to "put away all these" (Ephesians 4:31). Now, we can do just that.

If we put away evil doers, there are no more evil deeds. We may not achieve perfection...**but it will not be due to ignoring and not taking out** *the doers* **of the evil.** We can clean house and get as clean as possible...and remove all the true garbage. Remember: identify **the real problem, the real garbage**, and then remove.

It is not mine only. **The "sinful nature"** (a phrase that is not once found in the traditional Bibles/manuscripts and only found in the "modern bibles" of the last 130 years, based on mainly two faulty manuscripts but touted militantly as "the best", yet have 2,922 missing Greek words in the New Testament alone when compared to 97% of the extant manuscripts) is **from the original sinner and his spiritual army**, for he who sins is of the devil, **just as the holy nature is from the Holy One.**

We now see clearly, after having learned and after having our senses exercised to the discerning of good and evil. We need not try to control evil...**for we cannot control other beings.** We simply need to choose whom we will serve. **And then, we just reject and remove the enemy. Our real enemy. The evil dwellers of our flesh (Romans 7).**

We need to declare war...with understanding! And we now understand **the key**, and have proved it out...and it matches Scripture.

The key is: the enemy's army has been hiding in us, and through us, in "our flesh". The problem is not *only* **our flesh...is those that dwell in it and** *that influence and do* **the sin.**

Now that the eyes of our understanding have been opened, we see the simple solution, just as Yeshua purchased it for us. <u>Through Him and His name</u>, we can <u>cast</u> those evil dwellers <u>out</u>. Period.

Get rid of the "stink-ers"...and the stink is gone. Likewise, get rid of the "sin-ners"...and the sin also goes.

Now, we see.

Once we resolve <u>that we really do not want to have evil spirits manifesting through us, or</u> ***using us to do their dirty work***...**we simply stand guard, like never before, and take authority over them**, like the **watchmen we are called to be, over Israel and over our own lives, our families and each level in between. Then, we evict the intruders**.

How? We do this in the Name above all Names, in the power and authority that He has, and triumphed in, and gave us to do <u>even greater works</u> than those He did!

<u>**This is all just "Bible 101", but with eyes to see and recognize the true enemy and the true problem.**</u>

That is what He commanded us.

And, when we start walking in that mandate, boldly, **<u>yet humbly, transparent, in true repentance and brokenness, knowing</u> it is all from Him, and that we are simply His vessels, forgiven, cleansed, sanctified by Him, and yielded to Him AS TEMPLES OF ONLY HIS SPIRIT within us, <u>allowing no</u>**

others to dwell in us, THEN we will walk around this physical earth...even as Yeshua did!

And as we do, and walk in victory over the enemy, **we will also do this in unity with Yahweh and others, and in oneness...that which our brothers of Judah call "echad". When we do that**, we will be vessels meet for the Master's use (2 Timothy 2:21). And He will move us closer to achieving "the restoration of all things". We will walk in His ways and His Truth: **His "whole Truth". His Holiness, as He defines it.**

Why This Insight is Important

The reason we all, as believers, need to understand "the real problem" is that (as stated before) Yeshua came as the last Adam to solve the problem that resulted from the first Adam. **The real problem** is **that the enemy and his army**, the sin of Romans 5:12, **entered the world by the disobedience of** Adam. **And they have been doing so much stealing, killing and destroying, in so many ways, upon this world and upon all of us ever since**.

As stated in the introduction to this book, He absolutely set a time for everything...including His outpouring of this understanding and insight unto His people **so that we would see what we have not yet seen with enough clarity**.

And He set this time for us to see more clearly than ever that we have **not been recognizing the enemy enough**, that we have **not been removing him**

enough, and therefore, **he has remained in our midst far too much**, wreaking his evil work in and through us all.

The very Body of Messiah, which was supposed to go around exercising Messiah's authority over the enemy, **has been _spiritually_ sick and infected** with the enemy **enough that our work and "the Great Commission" has been greatly and severely hindered.**

This is why **this insight is being poured out by our Father**: **because if we do not remedy this spiritual infection from our midst, we will not be able to fulfill nor complete the tasks that have been assigned to us.**

But He WILL fulfill His Plan. And that is why He will accomplish **this "cure"**, this healing and restoration among us, using to a great extent these insights and understandings, **to give us the eyes to see and detect the enemy like never before, so we can then remove them and keep them from further hindering the Plan of the Ages.**

And, now He needs us to do it. Nay, He **chose** to include us in His plan of the ages. **We are included** in this thing called the restoration of "the Whole House of Israel", according to Ezekiel 37 and so many other Scriptures. Specifically, He is reuniting Ephraim and Judah...and the kingdom will no longer be divided but they shall be one unified kingdom...and He shall be the King of a restored and reunited Yisra'el.

Therefore, we, as His people on this earth and in His coming Kingdom, **have to "get our act together"**.

And He is the One who helps us. He is our Helper. He provides all things.

And what He is doing now is <u>showing us "the real enemy"</u> and <u>the real problem</u>. The problem is **everything that is not "pure and holy"**. <u>The problem is **the enemy and his army, opposing Yahweh and His plan**</u>.

It is certainly not a problem that worries Yahweh...not by any stretch. **What we do need to understand is that <u>these insights are Yahweh's agenda</u>. This is what Yahweh is focusing on and wanting to see come to pass. And it shall come to pass.**

The issue is: He is showing us His Truths and His purposes. <u>And, to do what He has called us to do, and "be about our Father's business", we are being called to walk in holiness and be holy as He is holy</u>. **Well, to do that, He is showing us that the invisible enemy has been wrecking His Body and witness on this earth for too long.**

He has appointed this time to show us how to recognize the enemy and his army. He is doing this **so that we might remove the enemy and his army from people's lives and from wherever we encounter them...just as Yeshua did** and demonstrated while He walked the earth.

<u>**This was how He brought the Kingdom of God**</u> on the earth. This was how He took authority **over the works** of darkness: **by taking authority and casting out *the workers* of darkness.** He cast the evil spirits *that were trespassing on God's Kingdom* and cast them out, to the dry places. By doing that, He

"destroyed the works of the devil", because for that purpose He was manifested (1 John 3:8).

He was like a "sheriff" from the Kingdom of God, saying "The Kingdom of God is nigh unto you" and He cast out evil spirits by the finger of God. **By casting the evil spirits that were trespassing on God's territory, Kingdom and people, He brought the order of the Kingdom, and the rule of the Kingdom, into manifestation**. And in that order, the people were healed and set free, like the daughter of Abraham that was loosed from the spirit of infirmity with which Satan had bound her 18 years...and she was straightened that very hour (Luke 13).

He was anointed of Yahweh and went about doing good and healed all those that were oppressed of the devil (Acts 10:38).

***Now, it is our turn*. It is our time to walk in an anointing and discernment greater than we have ever had in our lives; to walk in like manner to our Master and Teacher, Yeshua our Messiah.**

<u>That</u> is our Father's purpose and desire. He is **<u>now</u>** calling us to receive these insights, understanding and discernment **so that we can walk ahead and <u>be a</u> <u>people</u> that is *truly sanctified and purified* <u>through the discernment of, and *the removal of, evil presences</u>* in our lives and the lives of others.**

When we do that in our lives, and help others to do that in their own lives...**then** the Holy Spirit/Ruach HaKodesh will be **strong *and unobstructed* in us**, to lead us and guide us to all Truth...***and we shall truly be His people, and He shall be our God/our***

Elohim...and we will all have One King...and all Israel shall be saved.

May it be so, even in our day!

Father...move upon us and make us Kadosh l'Kha / "Holy Unto You"...and fulfill Your purposes...for each of us, and for Yisra'el...and for the whole earth.

Amein.

A Special Prayer and Moment of Decision

As I wrote these final words, I again sensed His presence upon me as at other times during the writing of this book. I understand that He desires to deposit a very special, tangible and distinct opportunity for many of you. **Read and discern whether this bears witness in your Spirit**....

*My prayer is that those of you who read this book and sincerely desire to do the Father's will, completely and unequivocally, in full surrender, in your lives and in the lives of others, for His glory and purpose, would receive, according to your desires and prayers to our Abba, a strong and powerful anointing upon your lives, the kind of anointing that only comes directly from Him, an anointing that is pure, and true, and genuinely from Him above...that you may do the greater works that Yeshua said we would do after His return to the Father...the kind of works that it will take, and that the Father has ordained for us to walk in, in these latter days and chapters of the final act...works that will be such in power and magnitude **to glorify Him**, that will amaze the world, as He promised they would be in these times. Know that the purpose is not for self...the purpose is for His purposes <u>only</u>.*

Friend, know that this power and calling is not for the casual seeker but for those that are ready, and have been prepared, and preparing themselves, for such a kind of calling and anointing as required by this, His calling to be His true people, His true remnant, on the earth, that will represent Him and truly be His vessels upon this earth and against the strong delusions and strong opposition that is coming upon the earth and upon God's people.

If that is you, then this prayer has been written for you.

As you read this, open your heart and being <u>to Him and Him alone</u>, He who knows and searches the hearts and tries the reins, to Him Who formed you and made you in the womb, the One Who will help you...and I now ask the Father, by His leading and direction, on your behalf, and I ask Him to reward you according to His plan for your life and the desires of your heart; that if you are at that moment, where you have been stirred in that special way, through the reading of this book, at the place that He would have you to be, I ask that He would bring it to pass now, and bring upon you all the revelation, wisdom, insight and true understanding that will make all of these things that were written here become as real and clear to you as He has, in His mercy, made to be for me.

I ask Him to empower you, as He has ordained for you, to become skilled in the discernment of good and evil, and to be transformed by the renewing of your mind; that the Word of God that dwells in you would become clearer, as He would have it become by His Spirit's work upon your life...and I ask Him to bring forth all the blessings that He has foreordained for you and your life, in order to bring about His calling upon your life and to successfully fulfill His calling upon your life...I ask that you release now, at this moment in my brother's/sister's life, everything which You have foreordained for this person to receive from You at this exact time and moment, which You saw and ordained since the foundation of the world.

And, I pray, even as Yeshua prayed, that You would sanctify him/her in Your Truth, and bless and keep, and cause Your Face to shine upon, and be gracious unto, and lift up Your countenance, and give him/her Your Shalom, in fullness and glory and mercy, that he/she may be kept safe by You, unto the fulfillment of his/her calling in Messiah Yeshua............in the Name of Yeshua our Messiah, we ask and pray.......

Amein.

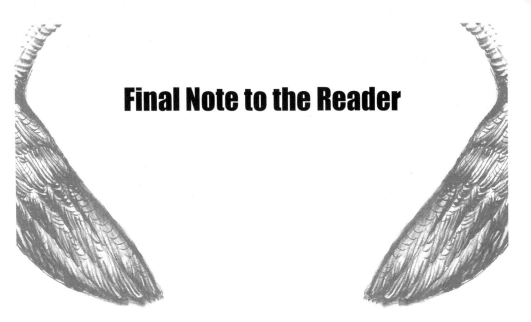

Final Note to the Reader

If you have been blessed and/or impacted positively through this book, I would like to hear from you.

Likewise, if you have any further questions as you honestly seek to understand what is presented here, I am accessible and willing to help.

I am also available for speaking engagements, teaching, training and/or ministry, as described in this book, to individuals and to congregations.

Please direct your emails to:

mdemelli@cfl.rr.com *or*
mdemelli@hotmail.com *or*
miguel@messianicisrael.com